D0577882

IN A WORD

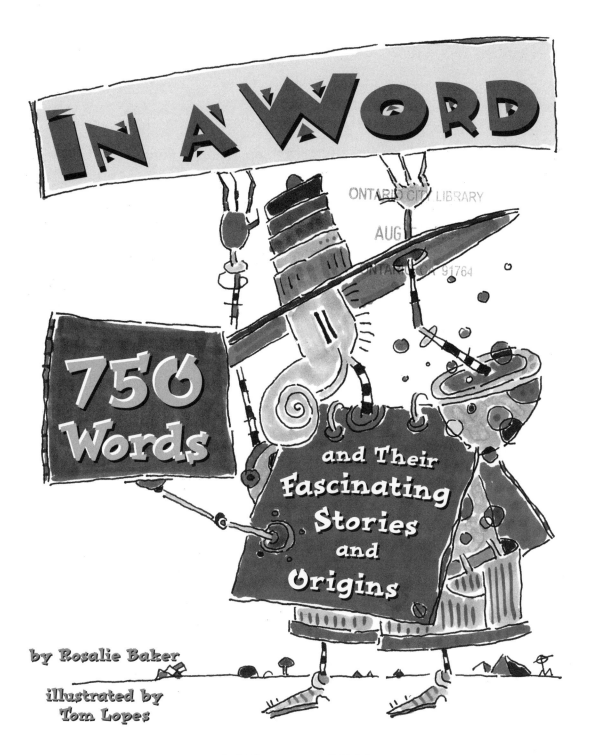

IN A WORD

750 Words

and Their Fascinating Stories and Origins

by Rosalie Baker

illustrated by
Tom Lopes

Cobblestone Publishing
a division of Carus Publishing Company
Peterborough, NH
www.cobblestonepub.com

For Charles Baker, Chip Baker, and Jennifer Parker
for their dedication and inspiration

Copyright © 2003 Carus Publishing Company

Printed in the United States of America

First American edition, 2003

Compiled by Chip Baker and Jennifer A. Parker

Designed by Ann Dillon

Copyedited by Meg Chorlian

Proofread by Eileen Terrill

The Library of Congress Cataloging-in-Publication data for *In a Word* is available at http://catalog.loc.gov.

Contents

Foreword

Words are slippery things. Words are also difficult to define. They fascinate me both for themselves and for the history they sometimes reveal. We all know what a cat is, but try to define the word "cat" without either pointing to a cat or using the word "feline" in the definition. Dr. Samuel Johnson in his great dictionary of the English language defined "cat" as: "a domestic animal that catches mice." Although his definition is true of most cats, it is not true of all; and there probably are other domestic animals that can be taught to catch mice.

Words are curious, often with curious histories, as you will learn from this book. Check out "candidate" or "senate," for instance. My wife remarked the other day that the day was "close." This sense of the word—hot and stifling—was popular in 1533 (and is in current use, but not commonly used). A person may be described as being "close with a dollar," which means that he is cheap, a skinflint, or stingy. We can see how this second meaning fits with our current belief about the meaning of "close"; but connecting the word to the weather or the atmosphere in a room seems a stretch. Words can be used to convey what we might think of as many different meanings.

Words are also extremely important. If we do not know the word for a *thing,* we cannot easily talk about that *thing*—without using the word "thing" or pointing or describing what the object is used for. We're forced to resort either to gesture or circumlocution (a lengthy way of expressing something). We cannot be ignorant of words connected with international relations or computers or the national economy or the life of the mind. If we are, we will find ourselves unable to take part in discussions of matters important to ourselves and to society.

I recently saw the word "donator" in a local paper. We all know what the word must mean, and we know that it refers to the person who donates. But does it exist in the English language? One of my dictionaries cites it, another does not. Which are we to believe? English possesses a perfectly good word ("donor") that would seem to serve the purpose intended; or is there some distinction to be made between a (possibly one-time) "donator" and a (regular and systematic) "donor"? I do not know, and will have to wait and see.

In addition to being important, the study of words is exciting, as you will discover by reading this book. From it you will learn about many words and their history, a history that is sometimes interesting and unexpected, as with the phrase "meet the deadline." Through these words and others you will marvel at human creativity, improve your vocabulary, and have a lot of fun.

Dr. William F. Wyatt
Professor of Classics, Emeritus
Brown University

Introduction

Every since my first week in 9th-grade Latin class, I have
enjoyed dissecting words. I enjoyed learning just what words
really mean and how these meanings had evolved. I already
spoke English and Portuguese, so Latin seemed to fill a "gap"
of understanding. It allowed me to see the relationships between
words and the people who speak them today, and the people
who used them in the past. My love of languages continued
through high school and into college and graduate school. As I
studied French, German, and Greek, each again broadened my
perception of language and how words reflect a people's beliefs
and customs.

In 1981, when my husband, Charles Baker, and I started the
monthly magazine now called *Calliope*, we decided to include in
each issue a column on words and their origins. That column,
"Fun With Words," still appears in each issue of *Calliope* today.
"Fun With Words" became a mini-education for me as I
researched words in languages that I did not speak or read.
I had long known that "fossil" traced its roots to the Latin
noun *fossa*, which translates "ditch" and symbolized something
that had been dug up from the ground. But I had no idea that
"bandanna" and "bungalow" each traced its roots to Hindi, a
language spoken in India, or that "typhoon" was an adaptation
of the Chinese phrase *taifeng*, meaning "great wind." Another
surprise was discovering that the cloth named "mohair" was an
adaptation of the Arabic word *mukhayyar*, meaning "fine cloth."

It is a treat for me to research new words for each issue of *Calliope*,
but, as the years passed, I wanted to find a way to gather together
all I'd learned and pass it on to new readers. We decided to create
this book, which features not only a lively discussion of word

origins, but also new information that is related in some way to the word derivations on a particular page. We call these tidbits PS, as in "postscript" (you can see its origin on page 15).

Lou Waryncia, the editorial director at Cobblestone Publishing; Marc Aronson, the publisher of Cricket Books; Ann Dillon, the art designer at Cobblestone Publishing; and Carol Saller, editor at Cricket Books, encouraged me. I wish to thank all four for their support and input.

Just as the "Fun With Words" column cannot include all words related to the theme of a *Calliope* issue, so this book cannot include the origins of all English words and phrases. I have included my favorites and encourage all of you to use them as a starting point for investigating the fascinating history contained within every word we read and write. You will soon find that an awareness of what word or phrase is appropriate and effective in a particular situation gives you a distinct advantage in school, on the job, and with your friends.

This book is a result of my lifetime of journeying through the words we use into the lives and history of people all around the world. I hope it is also the beginning of your quest to look inside words to the stories they tell.

Rosalie Baker

Cultural Creations

Ever wonder how the word "orchestra" evolved to mean both the location of the best seats in a theater and a large group of musicians who play together? You may consider yourself a "maestro" of arts and literature information after you have read this chapter.

A cappella

This musical term, meaning "without accompaniment," comes from the Frenchman Martin of Tours. Around the year 326, 10-year-old Martin rejected the gods of ancient Rome to follow the beliefs of the growing Christian church. Martin later became a missionary in Gaul and, in 360, founded the first monastery there. Regarded as a holy man and a miracle worker, Martin was honored as a saint after his death. The chief officials of Gaul placed his cloak, considered a holy relic, in a small room in his church. The room became known as the *capella,* which is Latin for "little cloak." The guardian of the cloak became the *capellanus.* Religious services were held in the *capella.* While there was singing, no musical instruments were used in the *capella.* For this type of music, the Italians coined the phrase *a capella,* meaning "in chapel style." Other languages quickly borrowed the phrase to mean singing without musical accompaniment. The French later adapted *capella* and *capellanus* to *chapelle* and *chapelain.* In English, the words became **chapel** and **chaplain**.

Gaul refers to the area of present-day France, and parts of western Germany, northern Italy, and Belgium. The Romans under Julius Caesar conquered Gaul, which was inhabited chiefly by Celts, in the Gallic Wars (58–51 B.C.)

Alphabet

Unlike the English language, which uses a sound to represent each letter, the Greek language had a name for each of its letters. Appropriately, the Greeks combined the names of the first two letters of their alphabet—*alpha* ("a") and *beta* ("b")—to form *alphabetos,* the name they gave to their entire body of letters. English later adapted *alphabetos* to "alphabet."

Anthology

An anthology is a collection of works from many authors. This definition, however, understates the very descriptive literal translation of the term—"gathering of flowers or a bouquet of flowers"—from the Greek words *anthos,* meaning "flower," and *legein,* meaning "to gather."

Applaud

In ancient Rome, most comedies ended with an actor turning to the audience with the request *"Plaudite!"* ("Clap!"). The Latin verb *plaudere* originally meant "to strike" or "to beat." However, to more closely express the later meaning of striking one's hands together or clapping, the Romans prefixed their request with the Latin preposition *ad,* meaning "to," to create *Applaudite!* On occasion, an actor experienced a different type of clapping. If the spectators did not approve of his performance, they would *explaudere* or "clap him out of" the stage. **Explode**, an English derivative of *explaudere,* retained this ancient meaning until as late as the 17th century.

Artist

An artist is someone who is skilled in the fine arts—painting, music, sculpture, dancing, and poetry. The term comes from the Latin noun *ars* meaning "skill," "knowledge," or "profession."

Known as one of the greatest artists of all time, Leonardo da Vinci gave definition to the term "Renaissance man" by being a painter, sculptor, mathematician, scientist, and inventor.

Calligraphy

"Calligraphy" means "the art of beautiful writing." It traces its origin to *kalos* (Greek for "beautiful") and *graphein* (Greek for "to write").

Chiaroscuro

In art, chiaroscuro refers to how an artist treats light and shadow in a painting. Usually the contrast between the two areas is very pronounced. Many works by the renowned Italian artist Leonardo da Vinci feature this technique. "Chiaroscuro" is a combination of two Italian words, *chiaro,* meaning "bright," and *oscuro,* meaning "dark."

Easel

What do an easel and a donkey have in common? *Ezel* is Dutch for "donkey." It seemed natural to 17th-century Dutch painters to share the word for an animal that was accustomed to standing and bearing many burdens with the name of the three-legged stand that holds a painting.

Encyclopedia

An encyclopedia is a set of books that provides information about many branches of knowledge. The word comes from three Greek words—the preposition *en* ("in") and the nouns *kyklos* ("circle") and *paideia* ("education"). Tradition credits English statesman and scholar Thomas Elyot with coining the term in the early 1500s. Elyot was known for his keen interest in promoting the study of ancient Greek literature.

Epigram

Epigrams are witty and sarcastic short poems. The word is actually a combination of two Greek words: the preposition *epi,* meaning "at" or "upon," and the verb *graphein,* meaning "to write." Other English derivatives of *graphein* are **graphic** ("of or relating to something written") and **telegraph** ("a communications system connected by wire that sends out and receives messages").

Comedy, in ancient Greece, dates to the sixth century B.C. The earliest comedy is Aristophanes' *Acharnians*.

Gargoyle

To decorate the cathedrals of medieval Europe, stonecutters carved grotesque heads of imaginary animals and detested political and religious figures and affixed them to rain gutters high above the ground. These heads caught the draining rainwater, which then spewed out from their huge open mouths. "Gargoyle" traces its roots to the Old French *gargouille,* meaning "throat," which is from the Latin noun *gurgulio,* meaning "windpipe" or "gullet." In later times, gargoyles became more decorative as greater emphasis was placed on the design rather than on the head's original purpose as a waterspout. *Gargouille* is also the root of the word **gargle.**

Glossary

Magazines and books that focus on a specific topic often include a brief section that provides a list of important words and their definitions. "Glossary" became a title for this type of section. It traces its origin to the Greek noun *glossa,* which first meant "tongue," and then also "language" or "word." The English language later adopted and adapted the term to mean "a collection of explanations."

incunabula

"Incunabula" refers to the first stages of anything. The word most often refers to books printed before 1500. The Germans coined the term, using the Latin noun *incunabula,* meaning "swaddling clothes." To trace its roots a bit further, *incunabula* is itself a combination of two Latin words, the preposition *in* ("in") and the noun *cunabula* ("cradle").

india ink

India ink is a solid black pigment that is mixed with a gelatin-type substance and dried into cakes or sticks. India ink was actually invented in China. After the 17th-century English government official Samuel Pepys used the expression "India ink" in his now-famous *Diary* to refer to deep black ink, the phrase was adopted into the English language.

italics

Francesco Griffo, the typecutter for Italian printer-publisher Aldus Manutius, first used a special slant-style typeface in 1501 for an edition of the works of the ancient Roman poet Virgil. The edition was dedicated in Italy, Virgil's birthplace, so the new typeface came to be known as *italics,* Latin for "pertaining to Italy." "Italics" is still used to refer to a typeface with slanted letters.

Both the *Divine Comedy* by Italian poet Dante Alighieri and *Paradise Lost* by English poet John Milton were modeled on Virgil's epic poem, the *Aeneid*.

Kabuki

Kabuki theater is a traditional popular entertainment in Japan. Its name—written using three modern Japanese characters—explains its form. *Ka* means "song," *bu* means "dance," and *ki* means "skill." Using elaborate costumes and staging, kabuki actors sing, dance, and perform in mime. This form of Japanese theater began in the late 1500s. Actors might stop a performance to address the audience. In turn, the audience answers or claps their hands according to a set of rules governing this behavior. Plays used to last an entire day.

Kindergarten

In 1837, German teacher Friedrich Wilhelm August Froebel coined the term "kindergarten" for the school he started for young children. Froebel's curriculum stressed the importance of play, family, pleasant surroundings, and nature. To name his school—the first of its kind—Froebel combined two German words, *kinder* ("children") and *garten* ("garden").

"Kindergarten" was also the name given to a group of young Oxford University students who aided British government official Alfred Milner in the reconstruction of South Africa following the Boer War (1899–1902).

Letter

Romans used the term *littera* to refer to the individual letters of their alphabet. They used the plural form of that word, *litterae,* to describe a letter written to another person. As *littera* passed through the centuries and was adopted by several European languages, its form was altered to conform to each country's spelling and speaking. But the variations in meaning between the singular and the plural forms were lost. In English, "letter" refers both to an individual alphabet letter and to a written message.

Maestro

Through the centuries, many Italian composers have been recognized internationally as outstanding musicians. Since most also taught or worked with the musicians who performed their works, they were called *maestros,* or "teachers." Today "maestro" is used to refer to masters in their area of music

Wolfgang Amadeus Mozart, one of the greatest maestros of all time, was born in Salzburg, Austria, on January 27, 1756. Reports indicate that when a cloth was placed on a harpsichord's keys, Mozart could place his hands under the cloth and play with the same precision and speed as if no cloth had been there.

Meter

Epic poems and other forms of poetry are usually written in meter, which means that the words in each line are carefully chosen and arranged to produce systematic and measured rhythms. Rhythms can be repeated, alternated, or changed completely to provide variety. "Meter" is derived from the Greek *metron,* meaning "a measure" or "a standard."

Musical terms in italian

Ever look at a page of sheet music and wondered what the "foreign" words found on the page mean? Known as musical directions, they are Italian words that tell the musician how the composer wants a section to be played. Some examples of this musical vocabulary and their English translations include:

al fine	continue to the end of a repeated section
allegretto	moderately fast
allegro	lively
andante	moderate in tempo
a tempo	in the original time (that is, before a change was indicated)
crescendo	gradually increasing in loudness
forte	loud
legato	smooth
lento	slow
lento molto	very slow
piano	soft
presto	quick
rallentando	gradually slower
rapidamente	quickly
scherzando	in a playful manner
staccato	in a disconnected manner
tranquillo	calm

Opera

"Opera" is actually the Latin plural form of *opus,* meaning "work." The first musical drama was given the Italian name *opera in musica,* meaning "works in music." In time, the phrase was abbreviated. "Opera" now refers to a play whose texts—solos, duets, choruses, and so on—are set to music.

Orchestra

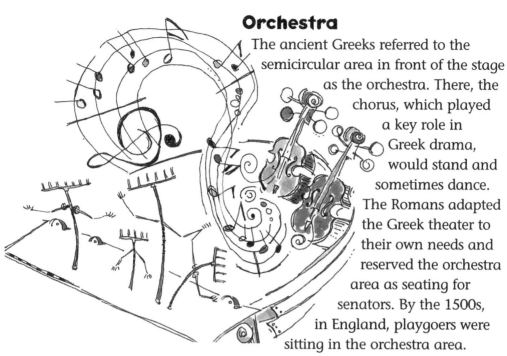

The ancient Greeks referred to the semicircular area in front of the stage as the orchestra. There, the chorus, which played a key role in Greek drama, would stand and sometimes dance. The Romans adapted the Greek theater to their own needs and reserved the orchestra area as seating for senators. By the 1500s, in England, playgoers were sitting in the orchestra area. At the same time, in France, the area was reserved for musicians. The English language borrowed both uses. Today, "orchestra" refers to both the best seats in a theater and to a large group of musicians that plays together.

Palette

To arrange and mix their paints, artists commonly use a palette, a thin board that sometimes has a hole at one end so it can be held with the thumb. The word comes from the Latin noun *pala,* meaning "spade" or "shovel."

Paragraph

In ancient Greece, punctuation marks did not exist. One letter followed another with no spaces between the words. To help readers, the Greeks adopted the practice of placing a short horizontal mark under the first word in the line where a new thought occurred. They called this line a *paragraphos* from their words *para,* meaning "beside," and *graphein,* meaning "to write." In English, "paragraph" is used to denote a subdivision of a chapter, an essay, or the like.

Philosophy

Philosophy refers to a particular system of principles for the conduct of life. A philosopher is one who studies or is an expert in philosophy. By origin, both "philosopher" and "philosophy" come from two Greek adjectives that imply a love of wisdom and knowledge: *philos* ("loving") and *sophos* ("wise").

Piano

When Bartolomeo Cristofori sought a name for his newly invented musical instrument about 1700, he chose the Italian phrase *piano e forte,* "soft and loud." He believed the characteristic feature of his invention was its ability to produce both soft and loud notes. These Italian words trace their origin to the Latin term *planus et fortis,* meaning "plain and strong." Today's simplified version—"piano"—has lost much of its original significance.

Plagiarism

There are strict laws against plagiarism, which is the disreputable act of using the works of another as one's own writing. Those who coined the term in ancient times used as its root the Latin noun *plagiarius,* meaning "a kidnapper."

Prima donna

This Italian phrase means "first lady" and is used to refer to the principal female singer in an opera or concert. The English language adopted the phrase and gave it the same meaning. The phrase is often used sarcastically to denote someone considered arrogant, vain, or very self-willed.

The first prima donna to gain the affection of the Phantom of the Opera on screen was May Philbin. She starred in the 1925 silent film of the story.

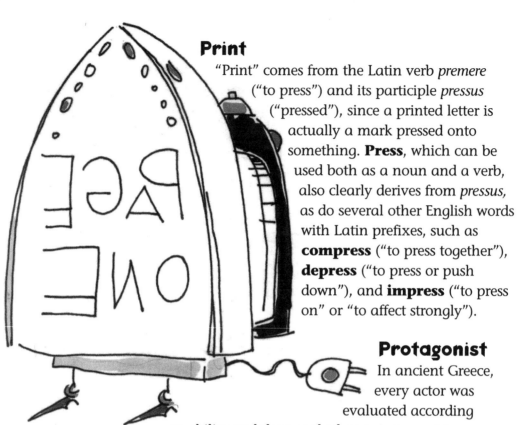

Print

"Print" comes from the Latin verb *premere* ("to press") and its participle *pressus* ("pressed"), since a printed letter is actually a mark pressed onto something. **Press**, which can be used both as a noun and a verb, also clearly derives from *pressus,* as do several other English words with Latin prefixes, such as **compress** ("to press together"), **depress** ("to press or push down"), and **impress** ("to press on" or "to affect strongly").

Protagonist

In ancient Greece, every actor was evaluated according to ability and then ranked as a protagonist, deuteragonist, and tritagonist. The prefix told the actor's position: *protos* means "first," *deuteros* means "second," and *tri* translates to "three." The "agonist" in each of the rankings traces its origin to the Greek *agein,* meaning "to lead." From *agein* came *agon,* which referred to a place into which men are led. In time, *agon* represented the great assemblies where the Olympic games and athletic and dramatic contests were held. The Greek noun *agonia* referred to the contest or struggle between the competitors or actors. The Greeks combined *agonia* with the appropriate prefix to classify the actors who performed on stage before an audience. The Greeks also used the prefix *anti* ("against") with *agonia* to form **antagonist**, which means "an adversary or opponent" in English.

Pupil

"Pupil" traces its origins to the Latin words *pupus* and *pupa*, meaning respectively "boy" and "girl" and making an appropriate term for "a student." Since the Romans considered a little girl and a doll somewhat similar, they used *pupa* for both. The Romans also noticed that when you look into the center portion of a person's eye, you see reflected a small doll-like image of yourself. They called this area of the eye *pupula*, "a little girl" or "a little doll." Two other English words that trace their roots directly to *pupula* are **puppet** ("an animated doll-like figure") and **puppy** ("a young dog").

Rehearse

The English word "rehearse" comes from the Latin word *hirpex*, meaning "a large rake." Since actors practice their parts again and again until they have mastered their lines and stage movements much the same as farmers rake their fields to prepare for cultivation, a combination of the Latin prefix *re* ("back" or "again") with a variation of *herce* (which is the French form of *hirpex*) were used to form "rehearse."

Sabbatical

In the field of higher education, a sabbatical refers to the leave of absence a professor may take. According to an old Hebrew custom, every seven years farmers were supposed to allow their fields a year's rest. *Shabath* was the Hebrew term for "rest" and referred to the seventh and holiest day of the week. Jews observe this period beginning at sundown Friday and ending at sundown Saturday (today's **Sabbath**). This practice followed the passage in the Bible telling how God created the world in six days and rested on the seventh. *See also* **jubilee** *(page 54).*

Schedule

In ancient times, the Egyptians, Greeks, and Romans used strips of the pith (interior) of the papyrus plant to form sheets of writing material. The Romans called the leaf of the papyrus plant *scheda*, a derivative of which was used to form the word *schedula*, Latin for a "small piece of papyrus paper." *Scheda* is a derivative of the Greek noun *schide* ("a split piece of wood") and the Greek verb *schizein* ("to split"). When *scheda* entered English, both its spelling and meaning changed, although not completely. The frequently used expression "on schedule" implies that someone or something has completed what has been written on a sheet of paper known as a timetable or a schedule.

Julius Caesar hired the mathematician Sosigenes to bring the incorrect calendar of his time into correspondence with the seasons. The new calendar had 365 days and was based on the Egyptian calendar. It also subtracted one day from February every four years—making what we now know as leap year.

School

"School" traces its roots to a Latin noun with the same meaning, *schola*. The Romans borrowed the Greek noun *schole*, referring to a group of young men who studied with a philosopher. The Greeks chose *schole*, meaning "leisure," because only those who did not have to work could afford to study.

Scribe

Using the verb *scribere* ("to write") as a base, the ancient Romans formed the noun *scriba* to denote a professional who copied texts. English adopted the term, changing the spelling only slightly. *Scribere* became the basis of other English words, for example, **description** ("a drawing of a picture using words"), **manuscript** ("an original text written by hand"), **subscribe** ("to sign one's name to the end of a document as an indication of approval"), and **postscript** ("a note written after the signature in a letter or at the end of a book or speech." Usually the note is preceded by the initials PS).

Statue

The Latin verb *statuere* means "to set up" or "to place." In English, "statue" came to mean "a work of art that was set up in a particular position or location."

Theater

This term traces its origins to the Greek noun *thea,* meaning "a look" or "a view." From *thea* the Greeks formed *theoria,* "a viewing," and *theatron,* "a place for viewing." The Romans borrowed *theatron* and adapted the spelling to *theatrum.* When the latter entered the English language, it was spelled "theatre" (still used in English today) before assuming its present form.

Violin

The name of this widely known and played instrument has an extensive history. It derives directly from *viola,* a stringed instrument that is slightly larger than the violin and tuned a bit lower. **Viola** comes from *viol,* a stringed instrument played with a curved bow that was used chiefly in the 1500s and 1600s. *Viol,* in turn, traces its roots through French and Old English to the Latin verb *vitulari,* meaning "to rejoice."

Yin/Yang

Sometimes symbols are used to replace words. When this happens on a regular basis, the words themselves are often forgotten. Such is the case with the symbol ☯. While many use this symbol as decoration or for other purposes, the symbol is actually the visual representation of the two forces known as *yin* and *yang*. According to Chinese philosophy, these forces complement and depend upon each other. When the two are in harmony with each other, they are seen as the halves of a circle—one represented as light and the other as dark. The small circles within each half represent that part of the opposite force that is always present in the other. According to Chinese philosophy, *yin* and *yang* are both found in every aspect of life. *Yin* tends to be dark and heavy, feminine and passive. It is also the quiet decay of autumn and winter. *Yang* tends to be light and airy, masculine and forceful. It is the new growth of spring and summer.

Worldly Words & Power People

Whether you are a "peasant" or a "barbarian," or are
from "Africa" or the "Arctic," your world—and words—
have a Greek connection. "Culture," however,
has more of a Latin beat.

Africa

In ancient times there was much trade between the lands with coastlines on the Mediterranean Sea. Although the Romans did not known how far the lands along the southern border of the sea extended inland, they knew well the hot, sunny climate of the area. They called the land *Africa,* most likely a derivative of their adjective *aprica,* which is Latin for "sunny." The Latin term can be traced to the Greek word *aphrike,* meaning "without cold." The Greeks also knew the hot climate of northern Africa.

Africa is the second largest continent in the world, second only to Asia. Thirteen percent of the world's population lives in Africa.

Arctic

To chart their course across the seas, the ancient mariners relied heavily on the stars, the movements of the constellations, and the position of the sun. To the north, they observed a group of stars whose configuration suggested the shape of a bear. To name this constellation, known today as Ursa Major (Greater Bear), the ancient Greeks used their term *arktikos* ("of the bear"). Through the years, *arktikos* came to refer to the northern regions of the earth. English altered the spelling to "arctic."

Barbarian

To the Greeks, all non-Greeks were *barbaros,* meaning "foreign" or "strange." While the origin of the word *barbaros* is still a mystery, many etymologists think that the term repeats the phrase the Greeks used to imitate the sound of words spoken by non-Greeks: *bar bar.* Today, a barbarian is someone who lacks culture.

Brazil

Early European explorers of the Americas discovered that the native people knew how to make a dye extract that produced bright red and deep purple colors. The dye used by the native Americans came from a common tree, known as the *brasil*. European merchants soon developed a great trade in brasilwood. As a result of the Treaty of Tordesillas in 1494, the Portuguese claimed the land where these trees grew and named the area *Terra de Brasil* or "Land of Red-dye Wood." Soon map makers and others began to refer to the land as *Brasil*. English later adopted the name and its pronunciation, only changing the spelling to include a "z" instead of an "s."

When Portuguese explorers led by Pedro Alvares Cabral claimed Brazil for Portugal in 1500, there were approximately two million native South Americans.

Canal

This English noun traces its roots to the ancient Greek noun *kanna*, meaning a "reed" or "tube." A canal, especially one that is small and narrow, resembles the long, hollow reeds that grow along rivers.

Cataract

Ancient Egypt was surrounded by natural boundaries: the desert to the west, the Mediterranean Sea to the north, and the Red Sea to the east. To the south lay the white-water rapids, or *cataracts,* of the Nile River. To the immediate south was the First Cataract, and beyond were five more cataracts. Throughout ancient history, few armies dared brave the quickly churning water found there to attack Egypt. When the Greeks encountered these rapids, they called them *katarhaktes*. Many believe this is a compound of the Greek words *kata* ("down") and *rhassein* ("dash").

Coast

The English language borrowed the Latin term *costa,* meaning "rib" or "side," to form the noun "coast." A person sailing along the coast is actually sailing along the side of the land.

Culture

Culture may be defined as the ideas, customs, skills, and arts of a people or group that are passed on from generation to generation. By origin, "culture" traces its roots to the Latin verb *colere* ("to take care of" or "to till the land") and its participle *cultus* ("planted" or "cultivated"). Thus, a people's culture includes all that a people have nurtured and practiced.

Delta

The Greeks gave the name *delta* to the fourth letter in their alphabet. The shape of a capital *delta* is a triangle. The Greek letter was eventually used to refer to the land feature that is formed from deposits of sand and silt at the mouth of some rivers, since they are usually triangular in shape.

Egypt

The ancient Egyptians often referred to Memphis, the religious center of the god Ptah, as *Hi-ku-ptah,* which translates as "mansion of the soul of Ptah." When the Greeks sought a word to refer to the lands along the Nile, they used an adaptation of this phrase, perhaps because they were familiar with the city of Memphis. In time, the Greek name, *Aiguptos,* came into English as "Egypt."

Cairo, the capital of Egypt, is the largest city in North Africa. The Egyptian ruler Menes is credited with uniting lower and upper Egypt into one kingdom around 3050 B.C.

Equator

Derived from the Latin adjective *aequus* ("equal"), the equator is an imaginary circle around the earth that is equally distant from both the North and South poles.

Ethiopia

The Greeks and Romans used the Greek name *Ethiopia* to refer to the land south of Egypt. It is a derivative of the Greek word *aethiops,* which translates as "land of the burnt faces."

Ethnology

Ethnology is the study of different cultures and the comparison of these cultures. The word "ethnology" is a combination of the Greek noun *ethnos,* meaning "nation" or "people," and *logos,* meaning "word," "thought," or "statement."

Foreign

This word traces its roots to the Latin *foras,* meaning "out-of-doors." Just as its roots imply, a foreigner is anyone who lives outside his or her own country, city, or homeland.

In ancient Greece, only men were granted citizenship. Women were considered to be under the care of men. In Greek city-states, foreign residents (both men and women) could acquire the status of *metics.* They had full civil rights, but they could not own property, legally marry a Greek citizen, or participate in politics.

Geography

The "geo" in "geography" traces its roots to the Greek noun *ge,* which means "earth." "Graphy" also traces its origins to a Greek word, *graphein,* meaning "to write."

Girl

Etymologists give several possible sources for the word "girl." One is the Latin noun *garrula* meaning "a chatterbox." It is from the Latin verb *garrire,* which means "to chatter and talk about nothing." Another is the diminutive form of the Greek noun *koure,* meaning "a young maiden." A third possibility is the Old English noun *girdle,* which meant "a piece of clothing worn by unmarried girls that was loosened at marriage."

Harem

The Arabic word *harim,* which means "forbidden" or "sacred," was first used to connote a holy place. Later, it came to designate the private area where women lived in a Muslim household. Entry into this area was forbidden except to a chosen few. The size of the harem and the number of women, especially wives, depended on the personality and resources of the male head of the household. The harem of most Ottoman rulers was enormous and ornate.

Lhasa, the capital of Tibet, also is known as the "Forbidden City." It earned this name because of its geographic inaccessibility (at 11,975 feet in the Himalayan Mountains) and because of the reclusive Buddhist monks who lived there.

infant

The noun "infant" comes from the Latin prefix *in,* meaning "not," and the Latin participle *fans,* meaning "speaking."

Khmer

"Khmer" refers to both the language of Cambodia and the people who speak it. "Cambodia" is the English translation of the Khmer word *Kampuchea,* which is a derivative of the Sanskrit word *Kambuja,* meaning "born of Kambu," and is also the name of a tribe in northern India. In the myth of Kambu, a *naga* ("serpent") king's daughter marries a foreigner named Kaundinya. To enlarge Kaundinya's land holdings, the *naga* king drinks the water covering the area, builds the newlyweds a capital, and changes the name of the land to Kambuja.

Kush

After 1550 B.C., the Egyptians often used the name *Kush* to refer to Nubia, especially Upper Nubia, an area located to the south of Egypt. The first mention of this name is found on an inscription dating to 1900 B.C. *See also* **Nubia** *(below)*.

Mediterranean

Known to the ancient Greeks and Romans as the Inland Sea because of its geographic location, the Mediterranean Sea was the connecting link in the trade routes of Greece, Carthage, Rome, and the Middle East. In the third century, this body of water was referred to as the *Mare Mediterraneum* (Latin meaning "Mediterranean Sea"). "Mediterranean" is a compound of the Latin adjective *medium,* meaning "middle," and the Latin noun *terra,* meaning "land."

Nation

"Nation" traces its roots to the Latin noun *natio,* meaning "a tribe," "a race," or "a people." To form this term, the Romans used their past participle *natus,* meaning "having been born," since *natio* implied a group of people born in the same area. English adapted the term and broadened its meaning to include various communities of people within one territory and under one government.

"Nationality" refers to the common characteristics that unite a people—language, country of origin, and the like.

Nubia

The exact meaning and derivation of this name is uncertain. In Egyptian, *nub* means "gold." Since Upper Nubia was known for its desert gold mines, there may be a connection. *See also* **Kush** *(above)*.

Orient

We use the noun "Orient" (with a capital O) to refer to the countries of East Asia, including China and Japan. It is not, however, an English word, but a Latin one. More than 2,000 years ago, the Romans coined this term from their participle *oriens,* meaning "rising." Each morning, they saw the sun, which represented life and good fortune, rising above the lands to their east. To refer to the lands west of Asia, the Romans borrowed the Latin participle *occidens* meaning "falling," because the sun set on the lands to the west. The English language also borrowed *occidens,* but spelled it with a capital O. **Occidental** refers to the part of the world west of Asia, that is Europe and the Western Hemisphere.

One of the world's most famous train runs was the Orient Express, which traveled a 1,700-mile route from Paris, France, to Istanbul, Turkey. The train ran from 1883 until 1977. It was restarted in 1982 traveling a different route.

Peasant

The phrase "ancient Rome" brings to mind an image of a civilized metropolis with majestic, marble buildings and temples. This, however, was the Rome of the emperors, not the rural areas or farmlands. The Latin adjective *pagus* first referred to a district or area removed from the city and then to the countryside itself. The noun *paganus* denoted a person who lived in the countryside under Roman jurisdiction. Used for centuries by the Romans, the term was adopted by other languages. The French kept its meaning, but changed the spelling to *paysan.* The English later borrowed this as the base for "peasant." While the spelling has changed considerably over the centuries, the meaning remains basically the same.

The Peasants' Revolt was a month-long uprising by English peasants and artisans in 1381. It followed the passage of a law imposing taxes on people rather than property.

Peking man

In 1929, fossilized bones belonging to a primitive human being were found near Peking (today's Beijing), China. Tests date the fossils to around 475,000 B.C. To label the type of early human who lived during that time, scientists coined the term "Peking man."

Peninsula

The two Latin roots of "peninsula" are the adverb *paene,* meaning "almost," and the noun *insula,* meaning "island." Thus, the word "peninsula" describes an area of land surrounded on three sides by water.

There are hundreds of peninsulas located around the world, big and small. Some of the larger and better known include the Scandinavian Peninsula, the Arabian Peninsula, the Yucatan Peninsula, the Florida Peninsula, the Korean Peninsula, and the Iberian Peninsula containing the countries of Spain and Portugal, which is commonly referred to simply as "the Peninsula."

People

In Latin there are three words that translate into English as "people." Each has its own distinct connotation and became the root of several English terms. To refer to human beings in general, the Romans used *populus,* meaning "the people." English derives a number of words from this root, including "people," "popular," "population," and "depopulate." **Popular** means "widely liked" and also "reflecting the taste or wishes of the people at large." **Population** is "all the people inhabiting an area." **Depopulate** means "to sharply reduce the population." *See also* **plebe** *(page 26) and* **vulgar** *(page 29).*

Plebe

To differentiate between commoners and aristocrats in Roman society, the Romans formed the term *plebs* to signify the former. *Plebs* became the basis of the English term "plebe" ("a freshman" or "a first-year student at the U.S. Military or Naval Academy"), as well as **plebeian** ("characteristic of commoners" or "unrefined in manners"), and **plebiscite** ("a direct vote by the entire electorate"). *See also **people** (page 25) and **vulgar** (page 29).*

Port

Cities that border rivers, seas, or oceans often become the area's major trading centers. The continued prosperity of such cities depends on the type of port each has. For example, a deep harbor means large boats are able to dock at the piers and unload their goods. Nearby forests mean a ready supply of wood with which to build trading vessels. In time, "port," an abbreviated form of the Latin verb *portare* ("to carry") became the term for a trading center. *See also **starboard** (page 130).*

The famous port city of Oporto, Portugal, whose name literally translates as "the port," gave its name to one of the country's major exports— port wine.

Public

The English adjective "public," which means "of or concerning the people," is a direct derivative of the Latin adjective *publicus* ("belonging to the people"). *Publicus* traces its roots to the Latin noun *populus* ("people"). Some additional derivatives of *publicus* are **publish** ("to prepare printed material for public distribution" or "to bring to the attention of the public") and **republic** ("a political order in which power lies with the citizens who cast votes for their representatives, who are, in turn, responsible to the citizens").

Pundit

Today, "pundit" means "an intellectual or stuffy critic or commentator." News reporters often refer to people who make judgments about national and international situations as political pundits. The word traces it origins to the Sanskrit term *pandita,* meaning "a learned man." For Hindus, **pandit** refers to a person who is well-versed in Sanskrit and the philosophy, law, and religion.

Refugee

"Refugee" is an English version of a French word. Its French root is the participle *réfugé* (meaning "taken refuge"), which, in turn, traces its origins to the Latin prefix *re* (meaning "back") and the verb *fugere* (meaning "to flee").

The Huguenots, a Protestant religious group, escaped from France to England to avoid persecution after the Revocation of the Edict of Nantes in 1685. They were the first group to be called refugees.

Rival

"Rival" traces its roots to the Latin noun *rivus,* meaning "stream." The ancient Romans called people who used the same stream *rivales.* Roman legal records list many court cases between *rivales* who found it impossible to settle differences concerning ownership of streams they shared. As a result, *rivales* quickly came to mean people who competed against each other for the same rights or objects. English adopted the term and its meaning, adapting only the spelling.

Sheik

A sheik is the chief of an Arab family, tribe, or village. The word is an adaptation of the Arabic word *shaikh,* which means "an old man" or "a wise man," which is in turn comes from *shakha,* meaning "to grow old." Since a person usually needs time to become wise, chieftains or sheiks usually were the elders in a community.

Sudan

An Arabic translation of the Greek *Ethiopia, Sudan* is a shortened form of *Bilad as-Sudan,* which means "land of the blacks."

Viking

Not everyone agrees on the origin of "Viking." Some believe the name is derived from the Old Norse word *vik,* meaning a "creek," "inlet," or "bay." Others see the English term *wic,* a derivative of the Latin term *vicus,* meaning "a camp." Temporary camps were a key feature of Viking raiding parties.

Villain

As ancient Rome grew in power and influence, wealthier Romans began to build country houses outside the city. In Latin, such an estate was called a *villa*. Caretakers, groundskeepers, and domestic help were needed to maintain the house and property, so the Roman landowner built other small dwellings around his large one. Eventually, this entire community was referred to as a *villa*. In time, any small community became known as a *villa* and the inhabitants known as *villani*. The early French adopted the term, changing the spelling to *villein*. During the Middle Ages, a *villein* was a free peasant or a common villager who owed allegiance to the lord who owned or was in charge of the area. Since peasant workers were uneducated and lived in rough dwellings, land-owners and others considered them to be crude and without morals. *Villein* gradually came to be associated with a person fitting that description and is used now to refer to a deliberate scoundrel capable of committing great crimes. English borrowed the French form as the basis for its words "villain."

Vulgar

The Romans used *vulgus* in a contemptuous manner when refer-ring to the lower-class, common Romans. Through the centuries, the meaning of "vulgar" has changed. Today, its first definition ("associated with the masses of people") has a negative connota-tion and more often it is used in the sense of lacking in taste. Also derived from *vulgus* are the English words **vulgarity** ("an act or expression that offends good taste") and **vulgate** ("the common speech of people, vernacular"). *See also **people** (page 25) and **plebe** (page 26).*

Math Magic
& Science Synergy

"A little staff or stick." "A star with long hair." "Eager to learn." Can you guess what words these definitions relate to? It won't be hard to "decipher" them. The answers can all be found in the pages of this chapter.

Algebra

A long time ago, the Arabic term *al jabr* was used to refer to the medical operation used to set broken bones. It means the reuniting of something broken. References in old texts also show that *al jabr* later came to refer to the process of putting numbers together. In the 16th century, the two words appeared in English texts as *algeber.* Within a century, *algeber* came to be used in its present sense, as the name of the branch of mathematics that includes equations and the relationships between numbers.

Ambulance

Today medical care is considered a priority in the United States and elsewhere around the world. But this has not always been true. Surviving written records from past civilizations reveal that care of the sick was not usually considered a priority. Sometimes a chronically or terminally ill person was just left to die. But on the battlefield, the situation differed. Because good soldiers were needed at all times and could not be allowed to die, wounds had to be treated quickly. Cities were usually some distance from the battlefield, so a temporary structure was set up nearby to care for the wounded. Since the unfortunate soldiers either walked or were carried in, the French called this type of early field hospital *hôpital ambulant,* or "walking hospital." *Ambulant* was a French derivative of the Latin participle *ambulans,* meaning "walking." English later adopted the term, eliminated the first word and changed *ambulant* to "ambulance." It now refers to the type of transportation used to transfer a patient.

The ancient Romans made steps toward medical progress in their time. They took care to avoid bad or night air—they thought it caused a feverish illness that they called *malus aer* ("bad air"). This reasoning proved correct, as it was later discovered that a type of mosquito often found in the night air caused what is now known as malaria.

Anthropology

Anthropology is the scientific study of the origins, behavior, and development of humans. The word comes from the Greek prefix *anthropos,* meaning "man" or "human being," and the Greek noun *logos,* meaning "word," "thought," or "statement."

Bacteria

Scientists in the mid-19th century looking through a microscope saw organisms that appeared to be little sticks. Following the tradition of the time, the scientists looked to Greek terms for a name for the organisms. Since *baktron* in Greek means "staff" and *bakterion* means "little staff or stick," *bakterion* was adopted and adapted to the English language. The singular form is "bacterium"; plural is "bacteria."

The first microscope was invented in 1675 by a Dutch inventor named Anton van Leeuwenhoek. By 1683, he had improved it enough so that he could see bacteria.

Center

The Greeks used their verb *kentrein,* meaning "to prick" or "to stick," to form the noun *kentron,* meaning "something sharp and pointed," such as a spur or thorn. *Kentron* also came to mean the specific area in the exact middle of a circle. As this area never moved, *kentron* came to represent the central point of a circle. The Romans adapted *kentron* to *centrum,* which in turn became "center."

Centralism is a political system that designates all the power to a central government.

Comet

"Comet" is from two Greek words. *Kometes* means "with long hair," and is derived from *kome,* meaning "the hair of the head." To name the stars that orbited the sun and trailed long, cloudlike tails, the Greeks used their noun *aster* ("star") and added *kometes.* This combination meant "a star with long hair" or "a star with a tail." The Romans borrowed *kometes* and changed the spelling to *cometa,* from which we get "comet."

The famous Halley's Comet is named for English astronomer Edmond Halley. Records dating back to 240 B.C. suggest that its sightings occur about every 76 years. It was last seen in 1986.

Crescent

There are several meanings for "crescent." One is a phase of a planet or a moon when it appears to have one concave edge and one convex edge. In ancient times, many of the peoples in the Middle East honored the moon in its first quarter (when it is shaped like a crescent) as a religious symbol. The rulers of the Byzantine Empire (4th to 15th centuries A.D.) adopted the crescent shape as their national symbol. Tradition says they did this because of the sudden appearance of a crescent-shaped moon that saved the empire from a surprise attack. Later, the leaders of the Ottoman Empire adopted the crescent shape as their national symbol. Since many of these rulers practiced Islam, the crescent also became closely associated with that religion. To name the crescent or C shape, the English language borrowed and then adapted the French participle *creissant* (meaning "growing"), which was itself a derivative of the Latin verb *crescere* ("to grow").

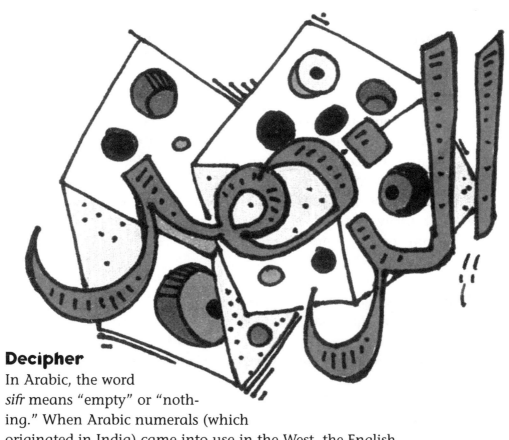

Decipher

In Arabic, the word *sifr* means "empty" or "nothing." When Arabic numerals (which originated in India) came into use in the West, the English adapted *sifr* to "cipher," a term that has a variety of meanings. These meanings include the number zero, the process of working mathematically with Arabic numbers, and a method of secret writing using characters of any kind. By adding the Latin prefix *de,* meaning "from" or "out of," English formed "decipher," or "to figure out."

Arabic versus Muslim versus Islamic: The word "Arabic" is used when speaking of the language of the Arab people. The term "Islamic" is used when speaking of the religion of Islam. The word "Muslim" is used when speaking of the culture and the people who follow the religion of Islam.

Electricity

The ancient Greeks did not discover electricity, but they did know that as you rubbed certain substances a variety of changes occurred. They especially were aware of what happened when you rubbed tree resin that had gradually turned to stone. Amber was their favorite hardened resin, attractive for its translucent color and its magnetic quality after being rubbed. The Greeks called amber *elektron,* from their word *elektor,* meaning "sunbeams" or "sun's glare." Many centuries later, when electricity was discovered, *elektron* was used as the base for the name of the science whose principals the ancients had first met in amber.

The first light bulb was produced by the English physicist and chemist Joseph Swan in 1860. However, the first practical light bulb that gave sufficient light for a sustained period of time was developed by Swan and U.S. inventor Thomas A. Edison in 1880.

Epidemic

The ancient Greek physician Hippocrates used the term *epidemos* to mean "to be among people" or "to be prevalent." This Greek term is a combination of the preposition *epi,* meaning "at," and the noun *demos,* which means "people." Today, an epidemic is a disease that spreads rapidly among people or animals.

Equinox

Twice a year the sun's rays cross the equator. Since day and night are of equal length at these times, the noun "equinox" and the adjective **equinoctial** were formed from the Latin words *aequus,* meaning "equal," and *nox* meaning "night." The equinox that occurs about March 21 is referred to as the vernal equinox (*vernus* meaning "of spring"). The equinox that occurs about September 23 is referred to as the autumnal equinox (*autumnus* meaning "of autumn").

Geology

The scientific study of the history of the earth, especially as it is found in rocks, is known as geology. The prefix "geo" is derived from the Greek noun *ge,* meaning "earth" or "ground." The Greek noun *logos* means "word," "thought," or "statement."

Geometry

Geometry means "to measure the earth." It was formed by joining two Greek words, *ge,* meaning "earth," and *metrein,* meaning "to measure." Such a choice was appropriate, since this science was first used to measure the land.

Euclid, the 3rd century B.C. mathematician, is credited with developing geometry. In his book *Elements (Stoichera* in Greek), he took earlier beliefs on the subject and developed the concepts and theories of geometry used today.

Hospital

"Hospital" literally means "a friendly place to rest." The Latin noun *hospes* translates as both "guest" and "host." The Romans believed that every *hospes* should be *hospitalis,* or "friendly." When they needed a term to designate an inn or hotel—a place where many people could stay and pay as guests of a friendly host—the Romans coined the word *hospitum.* Centuries later, there was a great desire among Europeans to visit Jerusalem and the Holy Land. These pilgrims were often poor and risked their lives on the journey. Around 1048, a military order of monks called Knights of the Hospital of St. John of Jerusalem established a hospital, or special lodging place, in Jerusalem. They began to welcome and treat the many pilgrims who arrived in Jerusalem in need of medical attention. Thus, we have the gradual association of a hospital as a place that offers treatment to the ill.

The Knights of the Hospital of St. John still exist as an organization today. The group's headquarters are in Rome.

Humor

The Latin noun *humor* translates as "a liquid." However, when used in the plural, *humores,* it refers to the four liquid fluids: blood, phlegm, bile, and black bile. The ancient Greeks and Romans believed these liquids were the key elements of a human being. The proportion of each fluid in relation to the others was what determined the health and personality of a person. Too much of any one *humor* radically affected the manner in which a person behaved. In English, "humor" came to mean "oddness," and a humorous individual originally referred to a cranky person. Gradually, "humor" and **humorous** referred to someone who made others laugh at the oddities of life. In ancient times, the terms coined to represent each of the *humores* became the basis for the terms describing the effect created by too much of that particular humor. An overabundance of blood made a person **sanguine**, that is, "warm, hopeful, or bloodthirsty" (from the Latin *sanguis,* meaning "bloody.") Too much phlegm made a person **phlegmatic,** or "composed or sluggish" (from the Greek *phlegma,* meaning "heat"). Too much bile made a person **choleric** or "hot-tempered" (from the Greek *chole,* meaning "bile"). Too much black bile made a person **melancholy,** that is, "gloomy or irritable" (from the Greek *melas,* meaning "black," and *chole,* meaning "bile").

Speaking of humor, the first comic strip appeared in the *New York Journal* on October 24, 1897. The strip was Richard Felton Outcault's "The Yellow Kid."

invent

This verb is actually an abbreviated form of the Latin past participle *inventum,* meaning "having been found" or "found." To form *inventum,* the Romans combined the preposition *in,* meaning "in" or "into," with their verb *venire,* meaning "to come."

George Washington Carver (1861–1943) invented dozens of uses for the peanut. These included grinding the nut into a powder, which was used to make soap, shampoo, and other products.

Mathematics

Because the early Greek thinkers saw numbers as a way to help them explain relationships, they spent much time developing formulas and equations. As a result, the Greeks used their adjective *mathematikos,* meaning "eager to learn," to name this new science. *Mathematikos* itself was a derivative of the Greek verb *manthanein,* "to learn."

It was Archimedes, the renowned Greek mathematician, who first calculated the approximate value of π, the symbol known as "pi" that represents the ratio of the circumference of a circle to its diameter as 3.14159265.

Medicine

Meaning "the science of diagnosing, treating, and preventing disease" or "an agent used to treat disease or injury," "medicine" traces its roots to the Latin *medicina. Medicina,* in turn, can be traced to the Latin verb *mederi,* meaning "to heal."

Physician

Just one of many medical terms that traces its roots to Greek and Latin words, "physician" comes from the Greek noun *physis,* meaning "nature," which in turn is a derivative of the Greek verb *phyein,* meaning "to produce" or "to become." **Doctor** is actually a Latin word, meaning "teacher." It comes from the Latin verb *docere,* "to teach." The status of a physician in ancient Greece was little more than a skilled craftsman. Physicians moved from town to town with their hired assistants.

Plague

"Plague" traces its roots to the Greek noun *plaga,* meaning "a blow." Latin adopted the word and added the meaning "wound." Today, a plague is a highly infectious, generally fatal, disease.

The Black Death was a plague that reached Genoa, Italy, on New Year's Eve 1347 and then spread across Europe and into England, Wales, Ireland, and parts of Scandinavia before entering Russia in 1353. It then spread into portions of Asia. Overall, the Black Death killed anywhere from one-third to one-half of all people living in these areas.

Planets

Ancient Roman astronomers named the five planets that they could see after their main gods (Mercury, Venus, Mars, Jupiter, and Saturn). Jupiter, the king of the gods, was used for the largest planet. Saturn, the god of agriculture and civilization, represents the second largest planet. The dry, red planet, is named after Mars, the god of war. The smallest and fastest moving planet is named for Mercury, the messenger god. The brightest planet is named for Venus, the goddess of love and beauty. Since the invention of the telescope in the early 1600s, three more planets were discovered and astronomers decided to follow tradition by naming them after Roman gods. The coldest, smallest, and farthest removed from the sun is named for Pluto, the god of the underworld. Uranus and Neptune are known as the "giant twins." Only Jupiter and Saturn are larger in diameter and mass. Uranus is named for the god of the heavens and grandfather of Jupiter. Neptune is named for the powerful god of the seas.

Plunge

To the ancient Romans, a piece of lead being thrown into the water made a sound like "plumbum." As a result, they called lead *plumbum*. Scientists later used Pb, the abbreviated form of this word, as the chemical symbol for lead. In Medieval Latin, the verb *plumbicare* described the act of lowering a lead ball into the water to check the depth. *Plumbicare* entered French as *plongier,* and is the direct root of "plunge."

Solstice

Twice a year, once in the Southern and once in the Northern Hemisphere, the sun is at its farthest distance from the equator. This is called the solstice. During these times, the sun appears to stand still in its southward and northward motion. Two Latin words were used to form "solstice"—*sol* ("sun") and *sistere* ("to stand"). In the Northern Hemisphere, the summer solstice occurs about June 21 and the winter solstice about December 21.

The equator divides the earth into the Southern Hemisphere and Northern Hemisphere, with the United States in the latter. When it is winter in the Northern Hemisphere, it is summer in the Southern Hemisphere, and vice versa.

Tantalum

In 1814, when scientists discussed what name would best suit a new element found in various minerals, "tantalum" was chosen. The reason: The element had proved "tantalizing" to those working with it because it was difficult to isolate and to extract from the minerals. "Tantalize" means "to tease or disappoint by promising or showing something desirable and then withholding it." It traces its origins to the mythological Greek figure Tantalus, whose punishment in the underworld was to have food and drink kept just out of reach. *See also **tantalize** (page 195).*

Religious Rituals,
Fabulous Folklore,
and Marvelous Myths

From the reverent to the far out and fictional,
here are some words that will explain how certain
religious terms and mythological mysteries
evolved into English.

Abbot

An abbot is the head of an abbey, a religious monastery or convent. The word traces its roots to the Aramaic term *abba,* meaning "father." Aramaic is an ancient Middle Eastern language and was spoken by Jesus, the founder of Christianity.

Altar

Many temples and churches have an altar—a raised platform where sacrifices, offerings, or ceremonies are performed during religious services. "Altar" is a derivative of the Latin adjective *altus,* meaning "high."

On September 15, 1853, Antoinette Brown became the first American woman to be ordained a minister. Her church was the First Congregational Church in South Butler, New York.

Amen

This is a Hebrew word meaning "truth" or "certainty." Originally used in the Bible at the beginning of a statement, it referred to a truth stated by another person. In Jewish tradition, however, "amen" was never used at the beginning of a thought, but rather at the end of prayers. In the Christian gospels, a double or triple amen was used on several occasions as a preface to stern sayings of Jesus. Christians expanded the custom, gradually closing every prayer with "amen," as a way of saying "thus it is" or "so be it" or "may it be so."

Ankh

The Egyptian word *ankh* refers to the hieroglyph the ancient Egyptians used to symbolize life on earth and in the afterlife. In form, the ankh resembles the letter "t" with a loop at the top. In temple and tomb paintings, Egyptian gods are often represented holding an ankh. Through the centuries, various organizations and groups have incorporated it into their own symbols. The Coptic Christian Church uses the ankh as a cross.

Apostle

"Apostle" comes from the Greek noun *apostolos,* meaning a "person sent forth." If we trace the roots of *apostolos,* we find it derives from the Greek verb *apostellein,* which is a combination of *apo,* meaning "from," and *stellein,* meaning "to send."

Atlas

According to Greek mythology, Zeus, the king of gods and men, waged war against his father, Kronos, for control of the kingdom. The battles were long and furious. Finally, Zeus and his allies triumphed. To prevent another such war, Zeus punished his enemies. Some he confined in the underworld. Others, he assigned very difficult tasks. The gigantic Atlas, for example, was sentenced to hold the world forever on his shoulders. In the 16th century, the Flemish geographer Mercator used an illustration of Atlas holding up the world in his book of maps. This book soon came to be called an atlas. In time, Atlas's name was used to label any book that illustrated the world through maps.

Baptize

The ancient Greeks used their verb *baptein,* meaning "to dip in a dye solution," to form another verb *baptizein,* meaning "to immerse." As Christianity spread around the Mediterranean world, Latin altered *baptizein* to *baptizare* and used it to refer to the religious ceremony where water symbolizes the cleansing or purifying of an individual and his or her entry into the Christian faith.

Christianity is the world's largest religion, with more than two billion members. Its branches include Catholic, Eastern Orthodox, and Protestant churches.

Belfry

During the Middle Ages, when rulers preferred to settle their differences on the battlefield, "berfrey" was an everyday word in England. At first, it referred to a moveable siege tower, then later to a fixed watchtower. One of the duties of the tower's watchman was to sound the alarm when an enemy attacked. To make sure all would hear the watchman's call, it became the practice to hang a bell in the tower. The close association of bell and tower resulted in a change of pronunciation from "berfrey" to "belfry." In time, "belfry" came to denote only a bell tower, especially the type attached to churches.

The Middle Ages was a period in European history that lasted almost 1,000 years. It began with the decline of the Roman Empire in A.D. 476 and ended with the growth of the Renaissance. *See also* Renaissance *(page 149).*

Bible

The ancient Greeks used the word *biblia* to refer to a collection of books. The word was actually a derivative of their word *biblos,* which meant "book." *Biblos* also meant "papyrus," a plant whose stem was used to make an early form of paper. Widely used throughout the ancient Greek world, the paper quickly came to be known as "papyrus." At the time, the Phoenician city of Byblos (in present-day Lebanon) imported and exported great quantities of papyrus. Thus, the Greeks began to use the name *biblos* as their word for "book"—the product of using many sheets of papyrus. In the second century B.C., Greek-speaking Jews used *biblos* to refer to their sacred writings. In the third and fourth centuries A.D., scholars of the Eastern Orthodox Church referred to their sacred writings as the *Biblos*—the "book of books." In time, *Biblos* became "Bible."

Caliph

A derivative of the Arabic term *khalifa,* meaning "successor," "caliph" is the title given to the successors of Muhammad, the prophet of Islam. These successors are considered the religious heads of Islam. From 1517 to 1924, the Ottoman rulers claimed the title of caliph.

Muhammad was born in Mecca in the year 570 and was orphaned before he was eight years old. Abu Bakr, Muhammad's closest friend and strongest supporter, succeeded him in 632.

Cemetery

All humans die. The most common final resting place throughout the world is burial in a cemetery. The root of the term is the Greek *koimeteron,* meaning "a sleeping place."

Christian

A Christian is a follower of Jesus, whose teachings form the basis of the Christian religion. Scholars believe he was born about 4 B.C. in Bethlehem, in Judea (present-day Israel), and died in the year 30. The area where Jesus lived, preached, and died is often referred to as the Holy Land. "Christian" comes from the Greek *christos*, meaning "the anointed."

The New Testament, one of two principal divisions of the Christian Bible, consists of 27 books. The oldest known surviving fragments date to about the years 120–130.

Cloister

A cloister is a place where a person may lead a life removed from the world, especially a monastery or convent. The word's history can be traced back to the French *clostre,* to the medieval Latin *claustrum* (meaning "enclosed place"), and to the Latin *claudere* (meaning "to close").

Religious Rituals, Fabulous Folklore,
and Marvelous Myths

Congregation

"Congregation" is derived from the Latin prefix *con,* meaning "with," and the verb *gregare,* meaning "to gather" or "to collect in a flock." *Gregare* traces its roots to the Latin noun *grex,* meaning "a herd" or "a flock." Today it commonly means a group of people gathered for religious worship.

Convert

When a person decides to turn from one way of thinking to another, he or she is called a convert. Usually, this refers to someone who has changed religious affiliation. The history of "convert" shows that it was coined from two Latin terms— the preposition *cum,* meaning "with," and the verb *vertere,* meaning "to turn."

Crusade

In the 11th, 12th, and 13th centuries, thousands of Christians marched east from western Europe. Their official goal was to retake Jerusalem and the Holy Land from the Muslims. To let everyone know that they believed in Jesus, who had died on the cross, they wore a red cross on their tunics and shouted as they marched into battle, "Take the cross!" In Latin, the term *crux* (the plural is *cruces*) meant "cross." Medieval Latin used *crux* to form the verb *cruciare,* meaning "to take the cross." Gradually, the words "Crusades" and "Crusaders" evolved to represent the Christian military expeditions and the individuals who participated in those marches.

When designing a coat of arms, Crusaders and knights used objects to symbolize qualities they admired or claimed to possess. For example, a castle expressed strength; a lion, pride; an eagle, swiftness; and a deer, grace and speed.

Days of the Week

The ancient Greeks and Romans named the days of the week after the sun, the moon, and the planets, which they had already named for their gods. The Germanic and Norse peoples adopted this practice and simply replaced the Roman gods' names with those of

similar deities. Six of the seven names for the days of the week trace their roots to Old Norse, an ancient Scandinavian language. In Old Norse, **Sunday** is *sunnudagr,* which means "sun's day." **Monday** is *manadagr,* "moon's day." **Tuesday**, *tyrsdagr,* comes from the name of the god Tyr, who is related to Tiw, the Anglo-Germanic god of war. **Wednesday**, *othinsdagr,* is connected to Woden, the chief Germanic god who is associated with Odin. **Thursday**, *thorsdagr,* is named for Thor, the god of thunder. **Friday**, *frjadagr,* pays homage to Frigga, Odin's wife. The exception is **Saturday**, named for the Roman god Saturn. The Old Norse name is *laugardagr,* "washing day."

The sources for Norse mythology are two books from Iceland that were compiled in the 13th century: the *Poetic Edda* and the *Prose Edda*. The first consists of poems about the myths and legends. The second is a more complete account of the myths, compiled by Icelandic statesman Snorri Sturluson.

Religious Rituals, Fabulous Folklore,
and Marvelous Myths

Fate

According to Greek mythology, three goddesses—Clotho, Lachesis, and Atropos—were believed to spin, measure, and cut the thread of life for each individual. In Latin, the idea of fate is usually found expressed by the term *fata,* the plural form of *fatum,* meaning "spoken." The Romans also used *fatum* as a noun meaning "a prophetic declaration" or "message from the gods." A frequently used Latin expression was *si fata sinant* ("if the fates allow"). Thus, "fate" traces its roots to the noun *fatum.* In art, Clotho is usually represented with a spindle; Lachesis, with a scroll or a globe; and Atropos, with a pair of scales or scissors.

Genie

"Genie" is the English transliteration of the Arabic word *jinni,* meaning "a demon." In Muslim folklore, a *jinni* is represented as a supernatural spirit that can take a human form and even influence human affairs. Perhaps the most familiar genie is the one that rushes forth from inside a special lamp, ready and eager to fulfill the owner's request.

To "transliterate" is to represent a word or phrase using the letters of another alphabet. To "translate" a word or phrase is to express the words in another language or in simpler terms.

Guru

In Hinduism, a guru, or spiritual leader, is a very important and revered individual. Because the Hindu religion is generally learned from a teacher rather than from books, the teacher becomes the focal point. A guru can help a person find the true nature within himself or herself. Today, people throughout the world use "guru" to refer to an intellectual or religious leader or advisor. Its root is the Sanskrit word *guruh,* meaning "venerable" or "heavy."

There are more than 750 million Hindus around the world. Hindus can worship anywhere. Hindu temples are not built as places for groups to worship, but rather as homes for Hindu deities.

Halcyon days

In Greek and Roman mythology, a king named Ceyx once ruled Thessaly, an area to the far north of the Greek peninsula. One day, he decided to brave the storms of winter to go to consult the famous oracle of the sun god, Apollo, at Delphi. Ceyx sought divine help, for his country had been beset by many evils for some time. His wife, Alcyone, begged him to wait until spring and better seas, but his sense of duty made him ignore her pleas. As the days passed and Ceyx did not return, Alcyone grew fearful. Hearing her prayers, the gods granted that Ceyx's shipwrecked body be carried home by the waves. Dreaming that her husband was dead, Alcyone ran from the palace and prepared to throw herself into the sea. Just then, she saw his body moving toward the shore. As she jumped to meet it, she felt herself change into a bird and saw that Ceyx's body was changing as well. The Greeks then adapted Alcyone's name to *halcyon* and the birds the couple became were thereafter known as halcyon birds (modern-day kingfishers). Alcyone's father, Aeolus, also wanted to honor his daughter. As the powerful god of the winds, he decreed that during the seven days before and after the winter solstice, no storms would stir the waters of the seas. This calm period would allow the halcyon birds to mate and bear their young. In time, the phrase "halcyon days" came to signify any calm and peaceful period.

Religious Rituals, Fabulous Folklore, and Marvelous Myths

Heretic

By definition, a heretic is a person, usually a church member, who opposes the beliefs and teachings of a particular religion. The English form of the word traces it roots to the Greek noun *haeresis,* meaning "a taking for oneself" or "a choice." *Haeresis,* in turn, is a derivative of the Greek verb *hairein,* meaning "to take" or "to choose." Hence, a heretic is one who chooses to take his or her own path. **Heresy** is the denial or deviation from orthodox religious beliefs.

icon

Derived from the Greek word *eikon,* meaning "image," "icon" refers to a representation or image of a person, usually in the form of a portrait. The term is frequently used in the Eastern Orthodox Church, where it refers to a painting, mosaic, or bas-relief (never a statue) of Jesus, his mother, Mary, or a saint. An **iconoclast** is a person who opposes the use of images to represent religious figures. Iconoclasts (from the Greek word *klastes,* meaning "one who breaks") often broke such images. They would substitute geometric patterns, plant and wildlife scenes, or Christian symbols such as a cross instead. Today, the word "icon" also refers to a picture logo on a computer screen. Click on the icon and a program opens.

"Iconoclasts" was a name originally given to followers of Leo III, emperor of the eastern Roman Empire, who forbade the worship of icons in the year 728. His decree led to the Iconoclastic Controversy.

immortal

This word traces its roots to the Latin prefix *im* ("not") and the Latin noun *mors* ("death"), or *mortis* ("of death"). "Immortal" is used to refer to someone who will never die. It also means "lasting a long time" or "having lasting fame."

islam

Islam is the name of the religion practiced by the followers of Muhammad, who are called Muslims. "Islam" is actually the Arabic noun form of the verb *aslama,* meaning "to surrender." Muslim people believe an individual is at peace only after he or she has surrendered to Allah, the Muslim name for God.

Islamic history and its calendar date from July 16, 622, the date of the *hegira*—when Muhammad, the founder of Islam, fled from Mecca to Medina.

Janus-faced

In Roman mythology, Janus was the god of beginnings and endings and of doorways. In ancient Rome, there was a temple dedicated to Janus. The doors were kept open in time of war to symbolize the help he gave. They were closed in peacetime. In art, Janus was always pictured with two heads, one facing forward to the future and the other facing backward to the past. "January" traces its roots to the name of this god, since January is the month that looks forward to the new year, but with memories of what has passed. In English, the expression "Janus-faced" has come to mean something deceitful and denotes facts that have a double meaning.

שַׁבָּת

Jubilee

A tradition among the ancient Jews (and still practiced by some Jews today) was the year-long celebration held every 50 years. This jubilee year came after seven sets of seven-year periods, followed by a sabbatical year (from the Hebrew word *shabbath*, meaning "to rest"). By custom, all those bound to a master and toiling his lands were set free, all mortgaged lands were returned to their rightful owners, and the land was left unplanted in the Jubilee. A blow on a ram's horn used as a trumpet signaled the start of the sabbatical year. In Hebrew, the word *yabel* means "ram." "Jubilee" came into English as the term for an anniversary celebration, in particular for the 25th or 50th. *See also* **sabbatical** *(page 13).*

"Hebrew" refers to the language used in ancient Israel and in the Old Testament. It was replaced by Aramaic beginning in the third century B.C., but continued to be used as a religious and literary language. Hebrew was revived as a spoken language in the 1800s and is the written and spoken language of present-day Israel.

Juggernaut

The Sanskrit term *jagannatha,* meaning "world protector," refers to Krishna, an incarnation of the god Vishnu, and to the images made of Krishna. Every year, in the town of Puri in eastern India, followers of Krishna drag a huge wheeled cart supporting a *jagannatha* through the streets. For centuries, many worshipers believed that whoever met death beneath the cart's wheels would join the god in his or her next life. On occasion, worshipers threw themselves beneath the wheels. The British, who occupied India from the 1700s through 1947, witnessed this ritual. They borrowed the term to form "juggernaut," which refers to a huge, overpowering, and destructive force or to something that requires blind devotion.

The god Vishnu is one of the Trimurti (Vishnu, Brahma, Shiva), considered the three principal divine forces of Hinduism. Vishnu is the preserver. He enters the world when evil threatens to overpower good.

Libation

In ancient Greek, the verb *leibein* means "to pour." The Romans adapted the form to *libare* and used it to mean "to taste" or "to pour." English then adapted the Latin form to "libation," meaning a ritual that involves pouring wine or oil as a sacrifice to a god. Today it also refers to an alcoholic beverage.

Magic

Persia was the ancient name for much of the area known as Iran today. In the Persian language, *magus* meant "priest," "fire worshiper," or "magician." The ancient Greeks adapted the term to *magos,* to represent a person skilled in the art of sorcery or magic, and then coined *magikos,* meaning "magical."

Mass

In the early days of the Catholic Church, the priest would dismiss those attending the service that included Holy Communion with the Latin phrase, *Ite, missa est,* meaning "Go, the meeting is sent or dismissed." In time, people began referring to the church service using only the word *missa* ("sent" or "dismissed"). Centuries later, *missa* entered Old English as *masse,* the root of "mass." Today, priests end the church service with the phrase "the mass is ended."

Missionary

This term traces its roots to the Latin verb *mittere,* meaning "to send," and its participle *missus,* meaning "having been sent." Throughout history, a missionary has been a religious individual sent to help the people in a foreign land and to convert them to his or her religion.

Christian missionary societies have existed since the era of European expansion in the early 16th century. Scottish missionary and African explorer David Livingstone was employed in Africa by the London Missionary Society. Although he made few converts, he actively opposed the slave trade.

Monastery

This noun and the name given to men living in a monastery—**monks**—trace their roots to the same Greek verb, *monazein,* meaning "to live alone." *Monazein,* in turn, comes from another Greek term, *monos,* meaning "alone." Usually, each monk has a very simple and plain cell-like room where he sleeps and prays alone within the walls of the monastery.

The Italian monk Benedict founded the Benedictine monastery at Monte Cassino, Italy, in the year 529.

Monseigneur

In French, *monseigneur* is used as a title of respect when addressing a ranking member of the court. This term, which is actually a compound of two French words, *mon* ("my") and *seigneur* ("lord"), traces its roots to the Latin adjectives *meus* ("my") and *senior* ("older"). In English, the title "monseigneur" (or "monsignor") is a religious title for a member of the Catholic clergy ranking above a priest but below an archbishop.

Monster

"Monster" is derived from the Latin noun *monstrum,* used to signify an important supernatural event. *Monstrum* was itself a derivative of the Latin participle *monitum,* meaning "having been warned," since the Romans believed that the gods created monsters to punish humans for their wrongdoings.

Mummy

The ancient Egyptians believed the spirits within a person lived on after death. Because these spirits had to be able to recognize the body, it was important to preserve the body and keep it from decaying. To do this, the Egyptians developed the process of mummification. "Mummy" is derived from the Arabic word *mumiya,* meaning "bitumen," a mineral pitch first believed to be the cause of the black pitch-like appearance of mummified bodies. Studies have shown, however, that bitumen was used in the embalming process only in late Egyptian history. Instead, the black look of the skin is believed to result from the oxidized resin (natural organic matter) used to coat the embalmed body and its wrappings. Nevertheless, "mummy" has continued to be used to refer to dead bodies that have been preserved by drying.

Muslim

This term means "one who submits to God" and refers to anyone who accepts and follows the teachings of Islam. The prophet Muhammad founded Islam. He was born around the year 570 in Mecca, in Arabia (present-day Saudia Arabia). His teachings, including his chief precept that Muslims should live in complete submission to God's will, are written in the Qur'an. The holy city of Islam is Mecca. *See also* **Islam** *(page 53)*.

Myth

"Myth" has changed only slightly from its Greek form, *mythos*, which means a "story" or "legend." Originally, a myth was based on some historical event and its author was unknown. Gradually, the definition changed to denote a tale about gods and goddesses. Today, its meaning is even broader and refers to any tale involving supernatural and/or exceptional happenings.

Greeks had no central collection of sacred texts, such as the Bible or the Qur'an. For them, this role was filled by an extensive collection of myths and stories about gods, heroes, and monsters.

Nemesis

The ancient Greeks believed in fate and worshiped a goddess who avenged extraordinary misdeeds and punished those who willfully and unjustly hurt others. In time, her name, "Nemesis," came to represent any person or act that avenges a grievous wrongdoing. According to Greek mythology, Nemesis was able to take many forms. Once, she changed herself into a fish to avoid Zeus. Today, "nemesis" describes a source of downfall or ruin or an unbeatable enemy.

Nirvana

The literal translation of this Sanskrit word is "the act of putting out or extinguishing." Buddhists use *nirvana* to denote the state of existence that occurs when an individual attains complete peace by ending all worldly desires and personal feelings. In recent centuries, the English language adopted the term to represent a goal that appears unattainable. English also uses "nirvana" to represent a state of mind or place where individuals have no cares and are completely happy.

To Hindus, nirvana symbolizes the extinction of the flame of life through reunion with Brahma. Buddhists see nirvana as enlightenment, a state of perpetual blessedness achieved through the extinction of all desires and passions. To Jains, nirvana is a state of eternal, blissful repose.

Noon

This term traces its origins directly to the Latin adjective *nona*, which was used to refer to the ninth hour of the day. Since the Romans set daytime hours as those from 6 A.M. to 6 P.M., the ninth hour was actually 3 P.M. As the influence of the early Christian church spread across the lands bordering the Mediterranean Sea, it adopted Latin as its language, the most widely spoken tongue at the time. To name the order of the prayers read by priests around 3 P.M., the church leaders chose the term *nones,* a variation of the Latin *nona (hora),* meaning "ninth hour." When the church leaders moved the time for the special prayers back to 12 P.M., they did not change the term *nones* because it was too closely associated with the prayers. In time, *nones* began to signify both the prayers and the time of day. Later, its form became "noon."

Omen

An omen is an occurrence that foreshadows some future event. The adjective "ominous" has a more sinister meaning, as it usually refers to the foreshadowing of something evil. "Omen" came into English without a change in spelling or meaning from Latin.

Oracle

In Greek and Roman times, certain areas were sacred to particular gods. Some sites were believed to be inhabited by the patron god or goddess. The ancients often traveled to these sites to ask the deity's advice. Trained priests and priestesses lived at or near the sites, and one of their religious duties was to interpret the wishes of the deity to anyone who came seeking advice. The Romans used the noun *oraculum* to refer to both the site and the methods that the god or goddess used to make known his or her wishes. English adapted *oraculum* to "oracle" and kept the same meaning.

The famous oracle at Delphi in central Greece was sacred to Apollo, the sun god. The "words" of the god were uttered by a priestess known as the Pythia.

Pagan

The Romans used the adjective *paganus* to refer to someone who lived in the village, such as a rustic or a peasant. They also used it to refer to non-military people, or civilians. The early Christians considered themselves "soldiers" of Christ, so they referred to anyone who was not a Christian as a *paganus*. Today, pagan still refers to non-believers, but more specifically to followers of ancient gods and goddesses that no longer exist.

Pali

Pali was the language used by Theravada Buddhists about 2,000 years ago. The Theravadins used it for their sacred writings and commentaries. "Pali" is a Sanskrit term meaning "row," "line," or "sacred writing." The language is no longer spoken. Theravada is one of two major schools of religious thought in Buddhism. It stresses that sorrow and suffering can be avoided only by ignoring desire. The other school is Mayayana, which stresses idealism, disinterested love, and relief of suffering of others.

Paradise

"Paradise" traces it roots to the Greek noun *paradeisos,* meaning "a park" or "a pleasure garden." To form this word, the Greeks borrowed an old Persian word *pairidaeza,* which represented the final resting place of those faithful to their religious beliefs.

Pastor

The word "pastor" is derived from the Latin verb *pascere,* meaning "to feed." Thus, a pastor is, literally, an individual who spiritually feeds his or her congregation.

Phoenix

In Egyptian mythology, the phoenix is a beautiful bird that lives in the Arabian Desert. Every 500 to 600 years, it sets itself on fire, and then rises from the ashes and begins life anew. Etymologists believe the word traces its roots directly to the Egyptian *bnw* (perhaps pronounced *boinew*), which is a type of heron sacred to the ancient Egyptians.

Pilgrim

Across medieval Europe to the Middle East, thousands of Christians made their way to visit the sites sacred to Christianity in the Holy Land. Such an individual was called a *pelegrin*. The roots of *pelegrin* can be traced to the Latin noun *peregrinus*, meaning "a foreigner" or "traveler from foreign lands." *Peregrinus*, however, was itself a derivative of two Latin words: *per*, meaning "through," and *ager*, meaning "field." In English, *pelegrin* later became "pilgrim," a term still used today to refer to anyone who travels in foreign lands, particularly to a shrine or holy place. **Pilgrimage** is used to refer to the journey made by a pilgrim.

The Pilgrims were a group of Separatists from the Church of England who left Europe to found a colony where they would have the freedom to practice their religious beliefs. They arrived in the area known today as Plymouth, Massachusetts, in November 1620.

Polytheism

Polytheism is the belief in many gods. It derives from the Greek adjective *polys*, meaning "many," and the Greek noun *theos*, meaning "god." **Monotheism**, which is the belief in one God, traces its roots to the Greek adjective *monos*, meaning "single" or "alone."

Priest

Presbys is the Greek adjective for "old." Its comparative form *presbyteros* means "older" and was used to refer first to the older members in a community and then to the older members in a church community. As centuries passed, speakers of Latin changed the Greek *presbyteros* to *presbyter*, but kept its meaning the same. *Presbyter* then traveled to France and became *prestre*. This French word then crossed the English Channel to England where it became "priest," an individual with the authority to perform religious rites. The French word also forms the base of **presbyterian**, meaning "a government of presbyters," or "rule by the community."

Reincarnation

A key Buddhist belief is that living beings, at the time of death, enter into a process of being reborn into a new body. "Reincarnation," the English word used to denote this process, is a combination of three Latin terms: the prefix *re,* meaning "again"; the preposition *in,* meaning "into"; and the noun *carnis,* meaning "body" or "flesh."

The Buddha's footprints are a common design symbol. They represent the continued presence of the Buddha's teachings after his death.

Religion

Only the letter "n" distinguishes "religion" from *religio,* the Latin word from which it is derived. Even the meaning of the two words is basically the same. The Romans defined *religio* as "reverence for the gods." "Religion" is a belief in a divine or superhuman power (or powers) to be obeyed and worshiped as the creator and ruler of the universe. Digging a little deeper, the Latin *religio* is itself a derivative. It traces its roots to the Latin prefix *re* ("back") and the Latin verb *ligare* ("to bind"). Thus the Romans saw *religio* as something that binds or ties a person to a defined set of principles. The same may be said of "religion." The world's religions with the largest numbers of followers are Buddhism, Christianity, Hinduism, Islam, and Judaism.

Sacrifice

The Latin term *sacer* means "set apart, holy, sacred." To refer to the act of offering something to the gods in petition or thanksgiving, the Romans combined *sacer* with *facere* ("to make") and formed the noun *sacrificium.* In English, "sacrifice" means "the yielding or giving over of one thing to gain another."

In ancient Rome, an appropriate sacrificial offering for Vulcan, the god of fire, was a red calf or boar. For Mercury, the messenger god, it was a male goat. For Diana, the goddess of the hunt, it was a young cow.

Religious Rituals, Fabulous Folklore, and Marvelous Myths

Sarcophagus

Upper-class ancient Greeks called their limestone coffins *lithos sarcophagos,* which literally means "stone that eats flesh." The phrase was coined because it perfectly described what happened to a dead body after it was laid to rest in such a casket. The chemical properties of limestone react with the human body and dissolve it. In time, the word *lithos* was eliminated and just *sarcophagos* was used. Today, limestone is no longer used for making coffins. Even so, the English language continues to use "sarcophagus," the Latin spelling of the Greek term, to denote a stone coffin.

The Egyptians also buried their dead in limestone coffins. On the walls of the coffins they would carve magic spells and prayers. According to the Egyptians, if the deceased recited these magic spells and prayers, the journey to the next world would be less strenuous.

Satan

This biblical term, which is used often in English to represent the devil, is actually a Hebrew word meaning "an enemy" or "an opponent." In the Talmud, a collection of writings that guide every aspect of Jewish life, Satan was an archangel who was cast from heaven because of disobedience and pride.

Swami

Swami is a title granted to respected Hindu religious teachers. The word traces its origins to the Sanskrit term *svamin,* meaning "master" or "owner." In English, the word also sometimes is used to refer to someone in authority who uses critical judgment in a particular situation.

Temple

Many etymologists believe that "temple" traces its roots to an unknown ancient word, the base of which was *ten,* meaning "to stretch." *Ten* traces its roots to the so-called Indo-European family of languages from which so many European and Asian languages, including Latin and English, are derived. The Romans used *templum* to designate an area in the sky that a soothsayer (a person who uses signs to predict the future) considered sacred by stretching out his arms. He then looked for signs appearing in this section in order to predict the future. As the decades passed, soothsayers and priests began using the same method to mark certain areas of land as sacred. Thus, the Romans began to call the building constructed on such a site a *templum.* English borrowed the term and changed it to "temple."

Greek temples are identified according to the style of their columns. The earliest and simplest column was the Doric, followed by the Ionic, and then the Corinthian.

Tree of life

A stylized tree is often found represented in ancient Sumerian, Assyrian, and Babylonian friezes. This tree, referred to as the Mesopotamian tree of life, is believed to have symbolized longevity and fertility. As a religious symbol, the use of a tree to represent life has continued throughout history. It has also been used to refer to the tree in the Garden of Eden, whose fruit offered everlasting life. Today botanists and gardeners use the Latin term for "tree of life," *arborvitae,* to refer to several species of evergreens and conifers of the cypress family. These trees are long-lived, retain their green needles year round, and produce abundant pine cones.

Whetstone

Whetstones are usually made of quartz and are used to sharpen knives or other cutting tools. According to Norse mythology, whetstones were made of pieces of the giant Hrungnir's club. In a duel with Thor, the Norse god of thunder and storms, Hrungnir threw his club at Thor at the same time that Thor hurled his thunderbolt hammer at the giant. The weapons met in midair. Hrungnir's club shattered into 1,000 pieces and fell to the earth, where they are mined in quarries to make whetstones.

Yoga

Yoga is a set of mental exercises and physical practices that originated in India. By following this training, students learn to remove themselves mentally from the world and unite themselves with the Absolute One. In Sanskrit, the word *yoga* means "union."

The *Yoga Sutras of Patanjali* is a Hindu classic that includes thoughts and practices with respect to yoga. Yoga became popular in the west as a means of relaxation, self-control, and enlightenment after 1950.

Exceptional Expressions

There is more than "a baker's dozen"
of sayings and expressions in this chapter.
You "know the ropes" by now, so let's
"call a spade a spade," and "ferret out"
how many of these sayings
are familiar to you.

Aboveboard

The actions of anyone walking or talking on the deck of a vessel are usually clearly visible. Below deck, however, in the passageways and dark corners, mutinies, smuggling schemes, and other plots can be hatched unseen. Thus, the expression "to be aboveboard" came to denote being honest, open-minded, and not concealing anything.

Achilles' heel

According to Greek legend, Achilles, the hero of Homer's *Iliad*, was the son of the sea goddess Thetis and the great-grandson of the king of the gods, Zeus. Achilles was renowned for his strength and bravery. His courage was partly due to his belief that no weapon could kill him. When he was an infant, his mother dipped him in the river Styx. Its waters made him invulnerable, but Thetis forgot to dip the one part she held onto as she immersed him—his heel. The sun god Apollo knew this and told the Trojan prince Paris. During the Trojan War, Paris shot Achilles in the heel with an arrow. The wound proved fatal. In time, the expression "an Achilles' heel" was coined to represent a person's or a nation's weak spot.

When Alexander the Great reached the shores of Asia in 334 B.C., he left his troops and took a side trip to Troy and the tomb of Achilles. There, he proclaimed himself the second Achilles.

Against the grain

The growth lines that run the length of a tree are referred to as the grain of the wood. Since ancient times, woodcutters and carvers have followed these lines to split, saw, and plane cut trees. Cuts that are made in this manner are smooth to the touch. Cuts that are made against the grain, however (for example, at right angles to the grain), are rough to the touch and usually produce slivers and splinters. The expression "to go against the grain" gradually came into use to represent the action of something that goes against what a person prefers or feels.

Apple of discord

According to an ancient Greek legend, the Trojan War began as a result of an apple thrown among the guests attending a wedding. Angered that she had not been invited to the wedding of Peleus, king of Thessaly, Eris, the Greek goddess of discord, entered the banquet hall and threw a golden apple into the crowd. When the guests read what was written on the apple—"For the fairest!"—three goddesses claimed the prize. They were Hera, the queen of Mount Olympus; Athena, the goddess of wisdom; and Aphrodite, the goddess of love and beauty. Paris, the son of King Priam of Troy, was summoned to settle the dispute. He chose Aphrodite, who had promised him the hand of the most beautiful woman in the world. Paris returned to Troy with his "prize" (Helen, queen of Sparta), but Helen's husband, Menelaus, was determined to retrieve his stolen wife. He gathered an army of Greek leaders and sailed against Troy. Today, the phrase "apple of discord" is used to refer to an object or incident that causes problems.

Babel

"Babel" means both "a confusion of sounds" and "the place where such confusion occurs." It traces its roots directly to the city of Babylon, which the ancient Greeks called Babulon. The Greeks had taken their name from the Hebrew name for the city, Bavel, which, in turn, traced it roots to the ancient Assyrian name for the place, *Bab-ili,* meaning "gate of the gods." According to the Old Testament, the people of Bavel wanted to build a gigantic tower to reach heaven. Displeased, God interfered and confused their speech. Instead of speaking one common language, the people of Bavel began speaking in many different ones. Work on the tower ceased because the workers could no longer understand and communicate with one another.

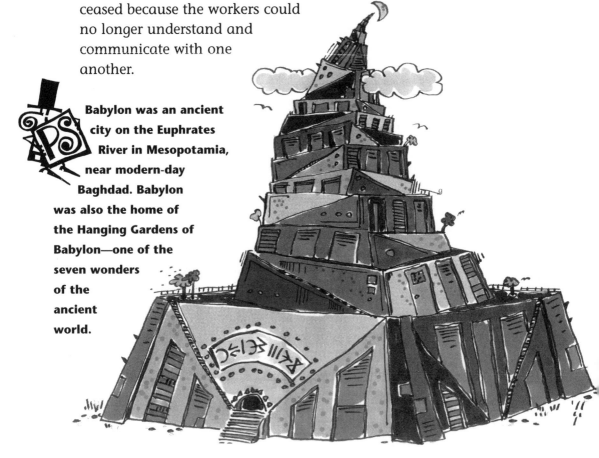

PS Babylon was an ancient city on the Euphrates River in Mesopotamia, near modern-day Baghdad. Babylon was also the home of the Hanging Gardens of Babylon—one of the seven wonders of the ancient world.

Baker's dozen

For centuries, bakers have known that increasing the number of air pockets in a loaf of bread makes the loaf larger. Since customers usually associated a larger loaf with more bread, some bakers took advantage of this fact and charged customers according to size, not weight. Around the 13th century, the English Parliament decreed that bakers were to sell their bread by weight and not size. Since it was almost impossible, at the time, to make sure a loaf weighed exactly a certain amount, many bakers decided to protect themselves by giving customers an extra slice of bread for every loaf they bought. A customer who bought a dozen loaves would receive a thirteenth loaf for free. Although scales and weighing procedures have improved, some bakeries still follow this tradition and give their customers "a baker's dozen"—13 items for the price of 12.

Beef up

The word "beef" comes from the Old French *boef,* which itself was a derivative of an ancient root meaning "ox," "bull," or "cow." We sometimes use the expression **strong as an ox**. Thus, "beef" also means strength. Since cattle are usually fattened before slaughter, "to beef up" came to mean "to increase or strengthen something."

Beware a wolf in sheep's clothing

According to tradition, around 600 B.C., a Greek named Aesop created a series of tales with morals or lessons. Animals representing human characteristics were usually the principal characters. One story told of a wolf who desperately wanted to have some sheep for dinner. To disguise his wolf-form, he wrapped himself in a sheepskin, entered the sheep pen, and ate his fill without being detected. Aesop's message was one that remains true today: Be careful of individuals who are not what they appear to be.

The first printed edition of Aesop's fables was in 1484, about 30 years after a German named Johann Gutenberg developed a new method of printing. Gutenberg is credited as the first European to print with movable type.

Beware of Greeks bearing gifts

The story of how the Greeks tricked the Trojans into bringing a huge wooden horse filled with armed Greeks within the walls of Troy was widely known to ancient Romans. When writing his epic poem, the *Aeneid,* the Roman poet Virgil used the style of Homer's *Odyssey* as his model. In a passage meant to convey the idea of deceit, Virgil wrote, "I fear the Greeks even when they come bearing gifts." Today, the phrase continues to be used by those who wish to caution others that there are some people who may outwardly express friendship but who are actually plotting the opposite.

In Book Two of the *Aeneid,* Virgil tells how the legendary Trojan prince Laocoön advised his fellow countrymen against bringing the great wooden horse within Troy's walls. Unfortunately, his advice was not heeded. The Trojans felt his advice went against the gods' wishes after they saw two snakes coil their bodies around Laocoön and kill him.

Beyond the pale

The Romans referred to the stake or boundary marker pounded into the ground to designate a county's borders as a *palus.* There were many of these stakes *(pali)* throughout the Roman Empire, including in England. English borrowed the term and the practice, adapting the Latin form to "pales," and used the stakes to mark the borders of the lands they took in conquest—Ireland, Scotland, and northern France. To be "beyond the pale" meant to be in land that was not ruled by England and to be beyond the reach of English law. In time, the phrase was used to refer to thieves and others who sought safety "beyond the pale." Today, it also refers to behavior that is morally or socially unacceptable.

The Romans conquered England in the year A.D. 43. The area remained part of the Roman Empire until the early fifth century.

72

Call a spade a spade

The first recorded use of this expression dates to the first century, when the Greek writer Plutarch included it in his biography of Philip of Macedonia (father of Alexander the Great). Writers and speakers through the ages have used the expression in its original sense: to refer to or to identify someone or something directly.

Catch a Tartar

While opinions vary about the origin of the word "Tartar," all agree that 13th-century western Europeans used the term to refer to invading Mongol tribes. The word was actually a derivative of the name the ancient Romans used to refer to Tartarus, the area in the underworld where evil people and monsters were sent for eternity. "Tartar," however, may have been chosen because of its resemblance to "Tatar," the name used to refer to several tribes that the renowned Mongol leader Genghis Khan conquered early in his career. According to tradition, when an Irish soldier was in battle with a Turkish soldier some time in the 1800s, the Irish soldier called out to his officer that he had "caught a Tartar." When ordered to bring him in, the soldier replied, "I can't. This Tartar won't let me." The story was repeated, and the expression "to catch a Tartar" came to represent a situation in which a person wins more than he or she can control. By itself, "tartar" is used to describe a violent, irritable, and stubborn individual. The word also describes hard deposits that form on your teeth. The origin of this meaning is uncertain, but may be linked to the Greek word *tartaron,* meaning "the dark underworld."

Chew the fat

When Christopher Columbus and his crew first arrived in the
Americas, they noticed that many of the native people chewed
the dried leaves of a plant that was unknown in Europe. They
also noted that some people placed burning leaves in a cylinder,
called a *tabaco,* and inhaled the sweet-smelling smoke by
sucking on the opposite end of the cylinder. A few sailors
experimented with the process, found they liked the taste,
and soon other sailors followed their example. The Europeans
quickly adopted the "chewing" and "smoking" habit. However,
since most boats were made of wood at that time, captains
forbade smoking the leaves on board. If the ship's store ran out
of tobacco leaves on a voyage, many sailors turned to chewing
leather strips, pieces of fat, or rags as a substitute. Because much
of the chewing took place when the sailors had free time, the
expression "chew the fat" was coined to refer to sailors
sitting around telling stories. In time, to "chew the fat" came to
mean sitting and chatting about nothing of great importance.

Curry favor

It has been standard practice for hundreds of years to clean a
horse by currying it—that is, by grooming it with a currycomb.
In 14th-century France and England, a fictitious horse named
Fauvel, the hero of the book *Roman de Fauvel* ("Tale of Fauvel"),
achieved great fame and popularity. He was, however, a sly and
deceitful animal. In England, the horse's name was Anglicized
to "Favel" and the expression "to curry Favel" became popular
to refer to a person who used lies and cunning to win another
person's attention and approval. "Favel" was sometimes
pronounced "favor" by those unacquainted with the French
novel and the horse.

Curse of the pharaohs

The pyramids of the pharaohs have fascinated and intrigued travelers for thousands of years. In recent centuries, many individuals journeyed to Egypt with hopes of uncovering mummies and other treasures. Yet, there were many individuals who advised against tampering with the tomb of a dead king. They believed the ruler's spirit would bring disaster to any intruder. Because disaster did strike on occasion, a pyramid explorer who suffered misfortune was thought to be a victim of "the curse of the pharaohs." Today, the expression occasionally is used when discussing people who involve themselves in projects that might cause them harm.

In 1922, the tomb of Tutankhamen was uncovered by Howard Carter and Lord Carnarvon. After Carnarvon's untimely death from an infected mosquito bite, Carter continued excavating the tomb for 10 years.

Cushy job

No one is exactly sure about the origin of this phrase. Many trace its roots to India. British officials and soldiers who were living there in the 19th and early 20th centuries often heard the phrase *hamari khush hai* ("it is my pleasure"). They soon adapted the word *khush* to "khushi," then to "cushy," and used it to describe a position or job that was not only pleasant, but simple and easy to do.

Cut the Gordian knot

According to Greek legend, a king named Gordius once ruled Phrygia (present-day central Turkey). As a gift to the gods, he dedicated his wagon to Zeus. Gordius then tied a very clever knot of cornel bark around the yoke. According to a local oracle, whoever untied the knot would conquer and rule the Eastern world. Many tried to untie the knot but failed. In 333 B.C., when Alexander the Great passed through Phrygia on his march eastward, he entered the old Phrygian palace where the yoke was on display and carefully examined the knot. He then pulled his sword from its scabbard and sliced through the twisted fibers. Ever since, "to cut the Gordian knot" has meant to solve a difficult problem with one dramatic stroke.

Dog days

In the Northern Hemisphere, July and August are the hottest months of the year. The ancient Greeks believed that the intense heat resulted from the fact that, during this period, the sun can be seen along the same celestial longitude as Sirius (from the Greek *seirios,* meaning "burning"). The brightest star in the sky, Sirius is a star in the constellation Canis Major ("the Greater Dog") and became known as the Dog Star. Gradually, the phrase "dog days" developed to refer to those days in July and August that are oppressively hot.

Archaeological evidence suggests that around 12,000 B.C. the Asian wolf was domesticated and became a companion to nomadic hunters living in Asia Minor— suggesting that the wolf, not the dog, was the first example of "man's best friend."

Feather one's nest

By instinct, many birds pluck the soft down from their breasts to make a comfortable, feathery lining for their nests. In 1590, the English poet and dramatist Robert Greene wrote, "She sees thou hast fethered thy nest, and hast crowns in thy purse." Thus came this expression meaning "to provide for one's comforts, especially by making money."

Ferret out

Sometime in the 10th century, European traders began importing small animals with pink eyes and yellowish fur from Africa. Because these creatures were quite tame and easily trained to hunt, the Europeans quickly saw their usefulness and taught them to hunt rats. To name their new "rat-catchers," the Europeans borrowed the Latin word *fur*, meaning "thief," added a suffix which implied "small," and formed the word "ferret." Soon the ferret was being used "to ferret out" all types of burrowing creatures, especially rabbits. In the 1800s, the English writer Charles Dickens first applied the phrase "to ferret out" to detective work.

Go berserk

According to Norse mythology, a fierce and reckless warrior named Berserk fought for Odin, the Norse god of war. Berserk and his equally savage 12 sons, known as Berserkers, entered battle dressed only in bear or wolf skins. The Scandinavians borrowed the name of these legendary heroes to refer to any fierce fighter. Gradually, the term came to describe anyone who became so reckless in his fury that he fought both friend and foe.

Grin like a Cheshire cat

The Cheshire cat in *Alice's Adventures in Wonderland* was described as disappearing gradually from Alice's view—with the grin being the last part of the cat to vanish. How the expression came about is unclear. Some say that originally the cheeses in the English district of Cheshire were shaped like cats that seemed to be smiling, since the district had special privileges, including the right not to pay taxes. Today, the expression means "to grin mysteriously."

Jig is up

The actual derivation of "jig" is lost, but most believe it came into English via the French word *giguer,* meaning "to dance," or from the French word *gigue,* meaning "a fiddle." Whatever the case, for hundreds of years the English have used "jig" to mean a lively dance. Around 1600, the English also began to use "jig" to mean "a bit of trickery." "The jig is up" grew to mean that one is no longer fooled, or that one knows about the trick being played.

Know the ropes

Just how this expression began is uncertain, but sailors were most likely the first to use it. Their job required a thorough knowledge of how each rope and line on their ship was handled. In time, others adopted the phrase and used it in a more general sense to mean being familiar with all the details of a particular situation.

Learn by heart

A common belief in ancient times was that the heart, not the brain, was the center of intelligence, memory, and emotion. Thus, when a person learned new material, he did so with his heart. This theory developed because the heart was the most noticeable of all internal organs. When the heartbeat stopped, so, too, did the person's life. As this belief was handed down through the centuries, "learning by heart" quickly developed to refer to the process of committing facts or words to memory. The Romans combined the prefix *re* ("again") with the noun *cor* ("heat") to form the verb *recordari,* meaning "to remember" and "to recollect." In 1374, the English poet Geoffrey Chaucer was the first to use the English phrase "learn by heart."

On December 3, 1967, the first heart transplant was performed by Dr. Christiaan Barnard. The heart of a 25-year-old accident victim was placed into the body of a 55-year-old grocer. The grocer lived 18 days before succumbing to pneumonia.

Leave no stone unturned

After the Greeks defeated the Persians at Plataea in 497 B.C., rumors spread throughout the Greek camp that the Persians had concealed a huge amount of treasure near the battlefield. Determined to find this treasure, their leader, Polycrates, sent a messenger to the Delphic oracle to ask what action he should take. The Greeks believed Apollo, the god of the sun and of predicting the future, would make known his wishes through a priestess. When Polycrates learned that the oracle told him "to leave no stone unturned," he decided to have his men turn over every stone in the area. Their efforts were rewarded, as they found the Persian riches. Today, the expression means to persist in seeking a specific goal.

Liar of the first water/First-class liar

For centuries, Arab gem traders carried on a large and profitable business selling precious stones, especially diamonds. Every diamond was examined and ranked according to its color and quality. It is believed that these traders compared a diamond's shine to the sparkling of pure, fresh water. By the 17th century, it was customary to classify the best diamonds as being "of the first water," the next best as being "of the second water," and so on. Although this ranking system no longer exists, the phrase "of the first water" has persisted as an expression indicating perfection in a particular area. Eventually, the word "liar" became attached to the phrase to refer to an extraordinary liar.

Lock, stock, and barrel

This American expression probably dates to the American Revolution and refers to the three most important parts of a gun—the lock, or firing mechanism; the stock, or handle; and the barrel, the tube, or cylindrical part. The three words together referred to the entire gun. Over time the phrase has come to mean the whole of anything.

Long time, no see

This expression is believed to have entered the English language from pidgin English. A pidgin language has no native speakers. Rather, it is a mixed way of speaking that incorporates words from one or more languages with the basic form of grammar from one of them. Pidgin English is a simplified form of English that was used by certain peoples of east Asia and the South Pacific in dealing with foreigners. "Long time, no see" is thought to be the pidgin English translation of the Chinese phrase *hao jiu bu jian.* Other pidgin English phrases are **chop-chop** (literally "quick-quick" or "hurry") and **no can do**.

Mad as a hatter

Today, we use this phrase to refer to someone who acts completely crazy. While its history is a matter of debate, a probable origin involves the trade of hat making. In the 1700s and 1800s, milliners (hat makers) treated felt hats with mercuric oxide, a chemical compound. Unaware that mercury fumes were poisonous, the milliners wore no protective covering. Over time, the fumes harmed their nervous systems, causing a loss of teeth, uncontrollable trembling, and other unexplainable behavior. Often, death was the result. Because no one at that time linked mercury fumes with the milliners' bizarre conduct, the expression "mad as a hatter" came into use.

In Lewis Carroll's famed novel *Alice's Adventures in Wonderland,* first published in 1865, the Mad Hatter is very impolite and very eager to confuse people with his mysterious riddles.

Meet the deadline

Reporters and authors know deadlines must be met for their story to be told. But today's deadlines are not the matter of "life and death" they once were. In the 1860s, at the Confederate prison camp at Andersonville, Georgia, the expression "deadline" was coined to represent a line drawn approximately 17 feet from the camp's fence. Officers on duty had orders to shoot any prisoner who crossed the deadline.

Out of the frying pan and into the fire

The idea this expression conveys—going from a dangerous situation to an even more dangerous one—dates back at least 2,000 years. The ancient Greeks used "out of the smoke and into the flame." The early Portuguese said "to fly from the frying pan into the coals." The French first used the phrase as we know it today during the 16th century, a time of great religious dissent.

Parting shot

Recognized as fearsome fighters, the ancient Parthians defeated many who attempted to invade their lands in what is today northwest Iran. The Parthians rode their horses into battle, shot a volley of arrows at the enemy, and then galloped away from a counterattack. As they withdrew they turned backward in their saddles to shoot another volley. The expressions "a Parthian arrow" and "a Parthian glance" developed to mean "a keen backward glance." In modern times, the expression "a parting shot" has become more common and refers to final, sarcastic words a person may use as an end to an argument or discussion.

Philippics

After Philip II gained control of his native Macedonia in the fourth century B.C., he looked south to the conquest of the prosperous Greek city-states. He began to forge alliances with some Greek leaders, but one Greek, a man named Demosthenes, was not deceived. Attempting to expose Philip's true intentions, Demosthenes delivered a fiery speech to his fellow Athenians. He urged them not to negotiate with Philip, but to defend their freedom on the battlefield. Failing to win public support for his views, Demosthenes waited. A few years later, he delivered a second passionate speech. Only after he delivered his third speech did the Greeks react, but Philip's well-trained troops still overwhelmed the Greeks. Demosthenes' speeches, however, were not forgotten and soon came to be known as the Philippics. Today, writers, journalists, and public speakers use the expression "philippic" to refer to a bitter verbal attack made by one person against another.

Pour oil on troubled waters

Roman writers of the first century suggested that sailors pour oil on the raging waters of a stormy sea to calm the waves. In time, the practice ceased. In the 1770s, Benjamin Franklin referred to this piece of advice in one of his works. A century later, when whale oil was used widely throughout the Western world, the idea of using oil to calm raging waters was once again promoted by some individuals. In time, the calming effect of oil came to be used as a metaphor and applied to people. In this case the oil represents whatever help or comfort a person may give to someone in a difficult situation.

Pull strings

In ancient times, hand puppets were a common form of entertainment throughout Europe. They fell into disuse in the early Middle Ages, but by the year 1000, their popularity had revived. The theme of medieval puppet shows was often religious and focused on stories from the Bible and lives of the saints. Instead of hand puppets, however, performers often used marionettes, which are elaborately carved little figures that are worked by strings. While the marionette was seen by all, the person who pulled the strings was not. Soon the expression "to pull strings" came to mean to influence from a distance.

Put the cart before the horse

Exactly when this expression came into use is unknown, but the idea of action against common sense dates back to ancient times and is found in writings thousands of years old. The phrase most similar to our English phrase was the one used by the Romans: *currus trahit bovem praepostere,* or "the cart drags the ox in the reversed order."

Red-letter day

The practice of using the color red to mark special holidays, festivals, and religious days on calendars began during the Renaissance. Since these times were usually joyful occasions, the expression "a red-letter day" came to mean "a memorable or joyous occasion."

Here's the word "red" in a few other languages: In French, it's *rouge;* in German, *rot;* in Greek, *kûkkivo;* in Italian, *rosso;* and in Portuguese, *vermelho.*

Red tape

From the 1700s through the early 1900s, red ribbon was used to tie official forms and documents in Europe. Cutting this ribbon took time, especially as it was often done slowly and according to special rules. To refer to the process, the expression "red tape" developed. The phrase continues to be used today to refer to the rigid application of regulations and routines that result in delays in getting business done.

Scot-free

"Scot" is an Old English word that is still used today to mean "a tax" or "a payment." The expression "to go scot-free" gradually evolved as a reference to someone who gets away without paying a tax or without punishment.

See red

This expression, which means "to be angry" or "to become angry," traces it origins partly to the long-standing association of the color red with anger and partly to bullfighting and the practice of waving a red cape to rouse the bull—even though bulls are color-blind.

Show a white feather

In ancient Egypt, Persia, India, and China, cockfighting was a popular sport. Gamecocks were raised and trained to fight against each other in a ring or arena. People in some areas of the world have continued this practice through the centuries. In the 18th century, some believed that if a cock had even one white feather, it was a coward and was sure to be a poor fighter. Soon, any individual who acted cowardly was referred to as someone who showed the white feather of his or her personality.

Slush fund

In the 19th century, cooks on ships used salt pork as a key ingredient for many meals because it kept well for long periods of time. When cooked, however, it produced large quantities of grease. The grease was then sold when the ship reached port, and the money used to buy small luxury items for the crew. This grease was called slush. The money earned from the sale of grease came to be called a slush fund. Today, the phrase is often used to refer to money used for  bribery, political pressure, or other corrupt purposes, or to unrestricted money obtained from a variety of sources.

So long

The actual derivation of this phrase is a matter of debate. Some trace its history to the Arabic greeting *salaam,* from the Arabic verb *aslama,* meaning "to seek peace." While *salaam* is an ancient greeting, records indicate that "so long" came into use only in the late 1850s.

Steer (sail) between Scylla and Charybdis

According to Homer, the hero Odysseus and his crew had to sail their ship between Scylla and Charybdis, two dreadful sea monsters. Many captains had tried the feat, but all had failed. Scylla was a dreadful sight as her six heads, each atop a long neck, emerged from a cave on a cliff overlooking the sea. Just across the strait churned Charybdis, a hideous whirlpool that three times a day sucked in and then spewed out the sea and all that happened to be in or on it. Only Odysseus survived the passage. He did so by clinging to a fig tree on one of the cliffs. The expression "to steer between Scylla and Charybdis" now means choosing a safe course between two equally dangerous or difficult choices.

Swan song

According to tradition, many ancient peoples believed that swans, creatures whose "voices" are not as melodious as those of other birds, burst into clear song when they felt death nearing. The fifth-century B.C. Greek philosopher Socrates is said to have explained that this voice transformation occurred because the swans were rejoicing. They knew that they were sacred to the god Apollo and that at death they would return to Apollo, who was the god of music and song. European literary tradition borrowed this thought, and the last work of a performer or artists is called a swan song.

Three sheets to the wind

The nautical term "sheet" refers to the rope or chain attached to the lower end of each sail. By pulling in or letting out on the sheet, you can control the angle of the sail. On very windy days, to ease the boat's heeling or tilting to one side because of the wind, sailors often loosened the three main sheets. The result was a vessel with flapping sails wavering on its course. Soon the phrase "three sheets to the wind" came to refer to anyone seen tottering along, especially someone who has drunk too much alcohol and cannot walk a straight line.

Turn turtle

Mariners use this phrase and the abbreviated form "turtled" to refer to a boat that has capsized and is floating helplessly upside down in the water. The source of this phrase dates to the days of the early mariners. On long voyages of exploration and discovery, sailors were always on the lookout for new food possibilities. The meat of the huge sea turtle was especially delicious. Catching these creatures, however, took skill and patience. The natives of the Caribbean islands were experts. They lay in wait as the female sea turtle came ashore to lay its eggs, then seized the creature by its flippers and turned it over, rendering the animal helpless. This method became known as "turning turtle." Soon sailors were applying this phrase to a boat rendered helpless because it had overturned.

Under the aegis of

"Aegis" is the English spelling of the Greek noun *aigis,* which referred to the short goatskin cloak worn by Zeus, the king of the Greek gods. By some ancient accounts, the skin had belonged to Amalthaea, the beloved goat whose milk had nourished Zeus after he was born on the island of Crete. Today, we use the phrase to mean "under the protection of."

The Aegean Sea lies between Greece and Turkey. Its southern boundary is the island of Crete. To the northeast, the Sea of Marmara links it with the Black Sea. The Aegean Sea is actually a part of the much-larger Mediterranean Sea.

Unstrung

Medieval English archers found that by using the yew (an evergreen shrub), they could make a bow that stood as tall as the archer himself. A yew bow also had enough power to send an arrow 100 yards and have its point enter an oak tree (one of the hardest known woods) to the depth of one inch. Unfortunately, this bow had one major disadvantage. When not in use, it could not be kept strung. The constant tension weakened the wood and, in time, prevented the bow from bending properly. Archers found it necessary to loosen one end of the bowstring on yew bows when they were not using them. This placed the archer at a distinct disadvantage. A yew bow required time to restring, a courtesy no enemy would grant. This fearsome prospect gave rise to the expression "to be unstrung." At first, it referred to a nervous archer with a loosened bowstring. In more recent times, it has been used to refer to anyone who feels extremely uneasy or fearful.

White elephant

In the southeast Asian country of Thailand (formerly called Siam), it was a national tradition to present the emperor with any white elephant that was captured. These rare elephants were sacred to the emperor. It was commonly believed that if the emperor became dissatisfied with one of his nobles, he would order a white elephant sent to him. Unable to use or destroy the sacred animal, the noble was forced to bear the cost of maintaining the huge beast. In 1629, the emperor of Siam sent King Charles I of England an elephant (records do not say whether it was white). The cost of its maintenance became a great drain on the royal treasury. Gradually, the phrase "white elephant" came to designate possessions that are expensive but useless.

Thailand is one of the world's major exporters of pineapples and natural rubber. Its capital city is Bangkok.

Work of vandals

The Vandals were a Germanic people from southern Scandinavia who settled on the south coast of the Baltic Sea. In the year 439, Gaiseric, king of the Vandals, took Carthage and drove out the Roman rulers. Sixteen years later, he and his troops sacked Rome itself. The Roman Empire in the West never recovered from this defeat, and as a result, the Vandals were feared throughout the Mediterranean world. Not until the late 1700s, however, was their name used to denote the willful destruction of property. A French bishop is credited with coining the term *vandalisme,* which entered the English language as "vandalism" and gave rise to this expression.

Worth one's salt

Because the Romans prized salt as much for its flavor as for its preservative qualities, they made it a rule that, as part of their pay, Roman soldiers would receive an allowance of salt or money to buy a specified amount of salt. This salt or money was called *salarium.* In time, *salarium* became the root of the English word "salary," and the expressions "worth one's salt" and "to earn one's salt" developed. *See also **salary** (page 201).*

Clothing Collection

You might not want to be seen in an outfit that includes "jodhpurs," a "bandanna," a "cummerbund," and a "poncho," but these words don't mind being seen together in this chapter that explains the roots of words for things people wear.

Bandanna

One of the methods used to dye cloth in India is known as *bandhnu*. It involves tying a piece of cloth in knots so that certain areas will retain their original color and not be affected by the dye into which the entire piece is being placed. When Portuguese explorers reached India in the 1500s, they purchased some of the material dyed in this fashion and referred to it as *bandanna*, their adaptation of *bandhnu*. English borrowed "bandanna." In time, the word expanded its meaning to include any large, colored handkerchief with a figure or pattern.

Buckle

For many Roman soldiers the most important piece of armor was their helmet. For hundreds of years, the basic style remained the same with only a few changes in the size and shape of the cheek plates, the nose guard, and the neck and shoulder guard. A welcome modification was the chin strap. Soldiers who fastened their straps securely greatly reduced the risk of losing their helmets in battle. Since the fastener that held the chin strap in place lay near or on a soldier's cheek, the Romans called it a *buccula,* meaning "little cheek." As the centuries passed, *buccula* broadened its definition and was used to refer to any type of clothes fastener. By the time English adopted *buccula* and adapted the spelling to "buckle," both the military connection and the association with the cheek had disappeared. The basic meaning, however, remained the same.

After a Roman soldier took his oath of allegiance, he was enrolled in the legion for 20 years. Upon completing the 20 years, he could retire on a pension and was given a piece of land in a conquered region.

Buff

In the western United States, buffalo hunting was common in the 19th century, and buffalo coats, called buffs, became popular. "Buff" soon became the term used to refer to the dull color of the undyed yellow hides. The verb "to buff" (to clean or shine with a treated cloth) traces its origins to the strips of buffalo hide that were used to polish metals such as bronze.

Caftan

Of ancient Middle Eastern origin, most likely from the area between the Tigris and Euphrates rivers in present-day Iraq, the caftan was commonly worn by Ottoman rulers. The basic design of every caftan is the same—a loose, ankle-length robe with long sleeves. Today, caftans can be found in almost any part of the world and in a great variety of colors and styles. Our English word comes from the Turkish *qaftan.*

The Ottoman Empire was at its height during the rule of Suleyman I (1520–1566). At that time, it included the Middle East, North Africa, southeast Europe, and the eastern Mediterranean.

Carat

Today, "carat" refers to the unit of weight—200 milligrams—that is used to measure pearls and precious stones, such as diamonds. Not so with the original "carat," which traces its roots to the Greek noun *keras,* meaning "horn." When the ancients sought a name for the seed of a carob tree, they adapted *keras* to *keration,* because the seeds look like little horns. Since carob seeds are all quite similar in size and shape, they came to be used as money. After being adopted and adapted into Italian and French, *keration* finally entered English as carat and is the accepted international jeweler's measurement today.

Cloth

Since early times, humans have used a variety of materials to fashion clothes for themselves. The word "cloth" comes from the Greek verb *clothein,* meaning "to wind thread." The names of some cloths trace their origins to names of areas or cities connected with the Silk Road. For example, **buckram** is coarse cotton or linen cloth from Bukhara, a city in Central Asia; **madras** is a fine, firm cotton cloth from Madras, a major city in India; and **shantung** is fine fabric made of silk from wild silkworms from Shantung, an older English spelling of Shandong, a province in northeast China. Other textiles trace their roots to languages spoken in the lands through which the Silk Road passed. For example, **mohair** is made of Angora goat's hair—from the Arabic *mukhayyar* ("fine cloth" or "choice"); **seersucker** is a light cotton, linen, or other crinkled fabric usually with a striped pattern, from the Persian *shir u sukkar* ("milk and sugar"); and **silk** is a soft, shiny fabric from *Seres,* the Greek name for the people from the East, the Chinese.

Cravat

During the Thirty Years' War (1618–1648), a regiment of mercenaries from Croatia (which was part of Austria at the time) fought for the French. By custom, each Croat wore a large, colorful muslin scarf that was edged with lace and tied loosely around the neck. The style caught on quickly among both the French soldiers and the French people, who began sporting scarves with long flowing ends. Since the French word for Croatian is *Cravate,* the French simply borrowed that word for the new kind of tie. When English adopted the custom, they used the same word, but dropped the last letter.

Cummerbund

Centuries ago in Persia (present-day Iran), men wore a cloth around their hips and lower abdomen (loins) that was known as a *kamarband.* This term was a combination of the words *kamar,* meaning "loins," and *band,* meaning "a strip of cloth used to bind something." English adapted this term and changed its meaning slightly. Today a cummerbund is still a band of cloth, but one that binds a person's waist.

Dungaree

Today, "jeans" is used far more frequently than "dungarees" to refer to pants made of coarse denim. "Dungaree" comes from *dungri,* the Hindi word for the material and also, according to some, the suburb of Bombay, India, where the cloth was first made. *Dungri* was used for making sails and heavy sheets. After it was introduced into England in the mid-19th century, a clothes manufacturer used it to make pants. Soon stores could not stock enough of the material. Another common material, **khaki,** also traces its roots to a Hindi word. When first woven in India, it was called *khah,* meaning "dust," because that word perfectly described the color of the material.

Levi Strauss was the first to patent jeans with copper rivets in the stress areas in May 1873. The traditional blue cloth used to make jeans was first exported from India to England in the 1830s. The cloth's durability satisfied the needs of the rough life of the California Gold Rush miners.

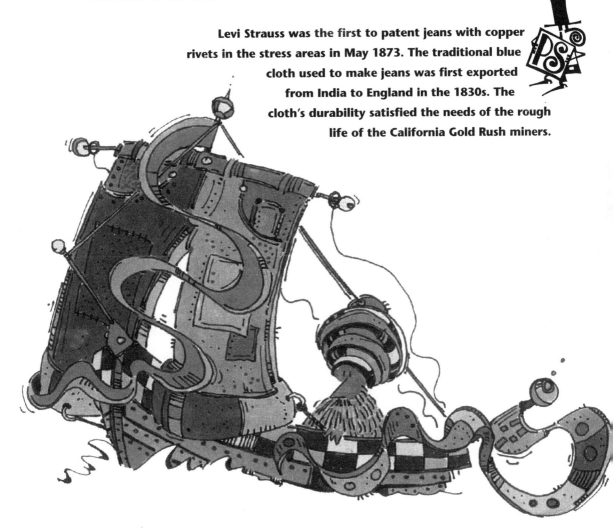

95

Jewels

As the cost of gold, silver, and precious gems continues to increase with each decade, no one today considers jewels to be of little value. Yet, "jewel" does trace its origin to the Latin noun *jocus,* meaning "a game" or "a trifle." "A little trifle" was *jocale,* a term the early French borrowed to form *joel* and *joiel. Joiel* later became *joie,* French for "joy." Hence, a jewel is something that gives joy and pleasure. Since jewels vary in value, a jewel sometimes is a mere trifle when compared to gold, silver, and precious gems.

Greeks often showed their reciprocal relationship with the gods by leaving votive offerings. The offerings were considered thanksgiving to the gods for past favors. Often, jewelry was offered to goddesses.

Jodhpurs

Jodhpurs are the pants horse riders wear. By design, they are loose-fitting and full above the knees and tight from the knees to the ankles. In the 1800s, British officials stationed in India brought them to England. The term traces its roots to the name of the area in northwestern India where they were traditionally worn.

Milliner

In the 1500s, many Englishwomen considered hats and dress trims imported from the northern Italian city of Milan to be among the best in Europe. In fact, the English called the people who sold these products "milliners," an adaptation of "Milaner," which was the English term used to refer to a person from Milan. Today, a milliner is one who designs, makes, trims, or sells women's hats.

Milan was first settled around 600 B.C. by the Romans. Later, under the emperor Diocletian, who ruled in the years A.D. 284–305, it was the capital of the western Roman Empire.

Pants

Medieval and Renaissance Italian comedy featured a stock character called Pantalone. A thin, foolish old man, Pantalone was constantly ridiculed. Dressed in slippers and wearing glasses, Pantalone always sported a special type of trousers that had long, fitted legs but a loose effect around the hips. In time, Italians began to use the name *Pantalone* to denote any comic character. Gradually, the term came to represent his trousers. In English, the word became "pantaloons" and was later abbreviated to "pants."

Poncho

The Araucanian Indians in Chile and Argentina, just south of the area inhabited by the Inca (present-day Peru), used *poncho* to refer to a cloak that was made of wool and had a hole in the middle for one's head. The Spanish borrowed both the term and the cloak. In the 19th century, it entered English without a change.

The Araucanian people offered strong resistance to the Spanish invaders in 1536. They managed to drive the Spanish out and reclaimed the land in Chile where their descendants still live today.

Raglan

A sleeve that continues in one piece from the wrist to the collar with no seams at the shoulders is called a raglan sleeve. The name traces its roots to the first Lord Raglan, the British commander in chief in the Crimean War (1853–1856), who was renowned for his courage and for the loose-fitting overcoat he wore on the battlefield with sleeves that extended to the neck. The style of sleeve became popular and was named for him.

Clothing Collection

Surplice

With no central heating and thick stone walls, churches and chapels in the Middle Ages were very cold and drafty. It became the custom for priests to wear a *superpellicium* under their official robes, especially in winter during long services. A combination of the Latin preposition *super*, meaning "over," and the medieval Latin noun *pellicium*, meaning "fur garment," *superpellicium* eventually lost its "fur" association. Nevertheless, when it entered the English language as "surplice," it did retain some of its original meaning. A surplice is an outer garment worn by clergy over their regular clothes.

Torc

Torc (also spelled "torque") is the twisted collar worn around the neck by ancient Gauls, Britons, and Teutons. It traces its roots to the Latin verb *torquere*, meaning "to twist."

Teutons are members of any Teutonic people, especially the Germans. They lived north of the Elbe River in Jutland, a region consisting of northern Germany and Denmark.

Glorious Gizmos & Great Grub

Hungry? We have on our menu "aspic," "syrup,"
"chop suey," "peaches," and "ketchup."
And our tour of these food- and house-related words
concludes with a dessert of "sherbet."

Alcohol

Many of the queens of ancient Egypt highlighted their eyes with a fine black powder, which they called *al-koh'l,* meaning "the fine black powder." Centuries later, the English language adopted the term and changed it to *alcool,* and used it to refer to any type of fine powder or extract (the essence of a liquid in its purest form). Only in the 1800s did the English begin to use "alcohol" to refer to the powerful essence in wine and liquor.

The first known wine grapes were grown in the Indus Valley around 4000 B.C.

Alcove

"Alcove" is actually a combination of two Arabic words: *al,* meaning "the," and *qubba,* meaning "vaulted room." During the Middle Ages, the Arabs ruled much of Spain, and many Arabic words naturally entered the Spanish vocabulary. Since many vaulted rooms at that time were small, the association of size and vaults gradually translated into the word *alcoba,* Spanish for "small vaulted area." The English later adopted the Spanish term, adapted it to "alcove," and modified its definition to mean a recessed area of a room that usually, although not always, has a vaulted ceiling.

Ammonia

The Egyptians considered the sun god, Amun, one of their principal deities, and four rulers bore the name Amenhotep, meaning "Amun is pleased." The Greeks considered Amun the equivalent of their chief god, Zeus, but spelled it Ammon. When the Greeks sought a name for the rock salt they imported from the area near a temple to Amun, they used *halas ammoniakos,* "salt belonging to Ammon." The Romans later borrowed the Greek term, spelling it *sal ammoniacum.* Scientists working with this salt in the 18th century continued to use the Latin phrase, but formed a new word—"ammonia"—to name the gas the salt produced. Today, ammonia is found in a great variety of products, including fertilizers, medications, and cleaning fluids.

Aspic

The French used the expression *frois comme un aspic* ("cold as an asp") to refer to a person with no warmth or feelings for others. The snake known as the asp, from the Latin word *aspis*, always has been feared because of its poisonous venom. When some French people used the phrase *frois comme un aspic* to refer to a popular type of cold jelly used to garnish fish or meat and the jelly mold itself, the word "aspic" was singled out as the name for that jelly.

Basin

Baca was the Latin word for "berry," and since the bowls the Romans used resembled the shape of a berry, later Romans coined the term *bacchinus* to mean "an eating bowl." During the Middle Ages, warriors used cone-shaped metal caps as helmets. Since this type of helmet was thought to resemble a bowl, the early French called it a *bacin*. English adopted *bacin* as "basin," a bowl-like container generally used to hold water.

Bin

The Celts used a term that sounded much like *benn* to refer to a special cart that carried a woven wicker form shaped to resemble a person. Some scholars think that people where placed within these wicker forms and then sacrificed by burning. English borrowed the term in the Middle Ages, adapted the spelling to "bin," and used it to refer to a manger or crib. Today, "bin" denotes a low container that is used especially for storing foods and other items.

The Celts were an Indo-European people who dominated much of western and central Europe in the first millennium B.C. They are famous for their rich mythology and for their art, especially pieces fashioned of metal.

Bungalow

"Bungalow" traces its roots to the Hindi word *bangla,* which refers to a thatched house. *Bangla* actually translates "of Bengal," an area in India where this type of one-story dwelling, usually with a wide, sweeping porch, was common. When the British controlled India, they borrowed the Hindi term and, in time, expanded its use to include any type of small, one-story cottage. In the United States, "bungalow" is used to refer to any small house or cottage.

Calabash

Since ancient times, many peoples have used the dried out shell of gourds to make drinking cups, dippers, bowls, and cups. "Calabash" refers to a type of gourd, and is a form of the Spanish name of the same fruit, *calabaza.* The Spanish were borrowers as well, for they took their word from the Arabic name for the same fruit, *qár'a yábisa.*

Gourds are hard-skinned, fleshy fruits from climbing plants such as squash, melon, cucumber, and pumpkin.

Candy

The root of "candy" can be traced to the ancient Sanskrit term *khanda,* meaning "a piece of crystallized sugar." The Persians modified the word to *kand,* or "sugar." Later, in Arabic, it became *quandi,* or "made of sugar." The term quickly traveled from the Middle East across the Mediterranean Sea, where it was adopted into several languages before coming into the English language as "candy."

The U.S. government was actually the first to invent the candy we now know as M&M's. The "melts in your mouth, not in your hand" candy was created as a quick-energy snack that would not get soldiers sticky.

Cane

Kanu, meaning "a reed," was a term commonly used by the ancient Akkadians. The Greeks adopted the term and adapted it to *kanna,* which the Romans later changed to *canna.* Sometime during the 14th century, the term was Anglicized to "cane." Although the term still refers to a type of reed, it more commonly describes an item used to help a person walk.

Canopy

For thousands of years, people around the world have used canopies—coverings set above a bed or throne or held above an important person or object. The English form of the word traces its origin to Greek. To refer to an Egyptian-style couch surrounded with mosquito netting (cloth gauze), the ancient Greeks coined the term *konopeion.* Whether the Greeks derived this term from *konops* ("mosquito"), or from *Knopos* (the name of an Egyptian town), is not known. The Romans borrowed the Greek term and formed *canapeum.* The French changed it to *canapé,* an hors d'oeuvre consisting of a cracker or piece of bread covered with some food. English also adopted the Greek term, but uses it only in the sense of "a covering."

Chair

Chairs were once costly items, bought and used by the very rich or by those in power. The most common type of seating, especially for large gatherings, was on a bench or on the floor. The ancient Greeks referred to a four-legged piece of furniture as a *kathedra*. It is a combination of *kata* ("down") and *hedra* ("seat"). The Romans adapted the term to *cathedra* and used it to denote the "chair of authority." Soon the phrase *ex cathedra* developed to refer to words or phrases that were spoken by someone in authority and that had to be obeyed without question. In medieval universities, the professor alone had a chair and the students sat on benches.

Today, universities have endowed chairs, or professorships, that are funded in part by donated money. Organizations also have chairs (sometimes called chairpersons) who are responsible for their continued operation.

Chiclets

The brand name Chiclets was aptly chosen to sell chewing gum. It traces its roots to *cikli*, a word long used by the peoples of Mexico and Central America to refer to a gum-like substance that is made from the milky juice of the sapodilla tree. Because it is a principal ingredient in making chewing gum, one company thought it only appropriate to call their brand of gum Chiclets.

China

The common noun "china" refers not to a country but rather to objects with a hard ceramic finish with a transparent glaze, or porcelain. By the 7th century, the Chinese had experimented with baking special clay at especially high temperatures to produce a refined, hard ceramic. The Chinese were the first to produce porcelain and, as the centuries passed, Chinese porcelain was exported around the world. To label the imported porcelain, the English used the name of the country where the ware originated. Today, the phrase "fine china" refers to extra-fine, quality dishes, while the term "china" has come to mean any type of ceramic dish.

Chisel

Although this word entered English by way of Old French, it actually is derived from Latin. Its root is the verb *caesum* meaning both "killed" and "cut." The French adapted the Latin to form their word *chisel,* meaning "a small instrument." English then adopted the French term, changing only the pronunciation.

Even though mechanical tools have made carpentry much more efficient, the chisel and other hand tools such as the awl are still widely used.

Chop suey

This Chinese American food dish is made by cooking meat and various vegetables together in a sauce and then serving the combination on rice. Although its name may look English, it is actually an English adaptation of the Chinese *zasui,* meaning "various pieces."

Chow mein

Supermarket shelves offer a variety of chow mein possibilities for shoppers. Most consist of a thick meat and vegetable stew that is flavored with soy sauce and served over Chinese noodles. "Chow" is an English adaptation of the Chinese verb *ch'ao,* meaning "to fry," and *mein,* the Chinese word for "flour." "Chow" also is heard every day in school cafeterias and military mess halls as a synonym for food.

Cocoa

The Maya and other peoples in Mexico and Central America learned to make a frothy, bitter chocolate drink from *kakaw* (beans from a tree native to the area). Since *kakaw* took much time and expense to process, laws were passed allowing only those of the upper classes to have this drink. Archaeologists have found *kakaw* recipes on vessels from the Classic Maya period (about A.D. 250 to 900). The Maya and others also used *kakaw* seeds as money. Spanish conquerors and settlers in the area adopted the practice of drinking this specialty and adapted the term to *cacao*. When the English language borrowed the term, it modified the spelling to "cocoa" and used it to refer to the powder made from *kakaw*.

American manufacturer Milton S. Hershey founded the Hershey Chocolate Corporation. He introduced the chocolate bar in 1894.

Cornucopia

According to the ancient Greeks, when Zeus, the king of the gods, was an infant, a she-goat named Amalthea nursed him. Later, when Zeus wished to express his gratitude to Amalthea, he plucked one of her horns and endowed it with special powers so that it would fill to overflowing with whatever Amalthea wished. Accordingly, the ancients represented it filled with Amalthea's favorites—fruits and flowers. The Romans borrowed this symbol of a horn overflowing with gifts of the earth. For them, it symbolized fertility and abundance. They named it the *cornucopia* from their nouns *cornu* ("horn") and *copia* ("plenty"). Today, it has become one of the symbols of our Thanksgiving holiday. *See also **Under the aegis of*** *(page 87).*

Crust

"Crust" refers to the hard, crisp, outer shell or covering of anything, but especially to the outer part of bread. It traces its origin to the Latin noun *crusta* ("the shell or bark of any substance"). Old French first adapted *crusta* to *croute,* from which English derived **crouton,** a small, crisp piece of toasted or fried bread used in soups and salads. The Latin *crusta* also gave us **crustacean**—animals with a hard, outer shell and jointed appendages that live in water and breathe through gills, such as lobsters, shrimp, and crabs.

"Crust" is not always used to describe food. For example, "the upper crust" refers to the elite or upper-class group of people.

Divan

The Turkish word *divan* traced its meaning to its Persian derivative and meant "a bundle of papers on which accounts were marked and kept." During the Ottoman Empire of the Turks, it meant the council of the ministers of state as well as the room in which they met. Since the council members sat on low, cushioned sofas that had no armrests or backs, this type of couch gradually came to be known as a divan. Westerners visiting Turkey and the Middle East quickly learned the term, brought it back home, and used it to mean a couch or a sofa. Westerners also used the name **ottoman** to refer to an armless and backless couch and later to a low, cushioned footstool.

Hacienda

This Spanish American term, used to refer to a large estate or establishment, comes from the old Spanish word *facienda,* meaning "work" or "an estate." The Spanish term traces its roots to the Latin *facienda,* meaning "everything that must be done." This adaptation was appropriate because on a hacienda, there is always much work to be done.

Ketchup

Also spelled "catsup," this English word is well known to all lovers of hamburgers, French fries, and baked beans. Few, however, know that it actually comes from two Chinese words. China's neighbors, the Malaysians, used *ke,* meaning "shellfish" or "seafood," and *tsiap,* meaning "a salty sauce," to form their word *kechap.* They then used *kechap* to mean "a fish sauce." European merchants trading in Asia in the 18th century brought the word home, where it underwent another change, first in spelling and later in meaning.

The first hamburger was invented in 1900 by Louis Lassen in New Haven, Connecticut. At Louis' Lunch restaurant, he served a boiled patty of ground beef between two pieces of toast.

Magazine

In Arabic, *al makhzan* means "a storehouse" or "a place where grain and other supplies may be stored." When the Spanish adapted the word, they kept the article *al* and formed *almacen* to mean a "warehouse" or "department store." English also borrowed *al makhzan,* dropped the article *al,* and adapted it to "magazine." English did keep the "storehouse" meaning, but also used the term to refer to books as storehouses of information. In the 18th and 19th centuries, when pamphlets and small publications became popular, "magazine" was gradually used to refer to these publications.

One of the first regularly published American magazines was the *Saturday Evening Post*. Founded by Charles Alexander and Samuel Atkinson, it first appeared in 1821 in Philadelphia.

Mansion

In Latin, the verb form *mansi* means "I stayed," "I remained," and, on occasion, "I spent the night." From it, the Romans derived their noun *mansio,* meaning "a stay," "a sojourn," or "a halting place." In turn, the English language derived "mansion" from these Latin forms. While its spelling has not changed, its definition has. Initially, it represented a dwelling place or lodging or apartment. In the 14th century, "mansion" was used to signify a journey, a halting place, and even the distance between two places. In the 15th century, it referred to the chief residence of a lord or wealthy landowner. As a result of the latter definition, "mansion" assumed its present significance in English as a dwelling of great size.

The ancient Romans had two kinds of houses: the *domus* (a single-family dwelling) and the *insulae* (apartment blocks or tenements). The rich lived in the *domi* (plural of *domus);* the poor in the *insulae*.

Onion

The Latin verb form *unio* traces its roots to the Latin adjective *unus*. The verb form means "I unite" or "I join," while the adjective means "one." When considering a name for the vegetable known as the onion, *unus* was used. What better term could describe this vegetable whose layers are so united? Another interesting note is the fact that the Romans used *unio* for a single large pearl. The English language borrowed this sense as well—the small silvery-white onions you buy in a grocery store are referred to as pearl onions.

Palace

Rome was founded on the hilly left bank of the Tiber River. Gradually, the phrase "seven hills of Rome" was used to describe the site. As Rome grew and its population gradually covered the surrounding hills, the Palatine Hill was preferred by Rome's wealthier citizens. In time, the emperor's residence covered almost the entire hill. The French adapted the name Palatine to *palais* and used it to represent their king's official residence. English changed the French term to "palace."

When the Roman emperor Nero (54–68) ordered construction of his Golden House in Rome, he wanted to create the effect of a city palace in the country. It was massive and even included a swimming pool.

Pasta

The Italian word *pasta* is found on restaurant menus and in super-markets around the world. In fact, pasta has become one of the world's most popular foods. The term traces its roots through the Greek noun *paste,* meaning "barley porridge," to the Greek verb *passein,* meaning "to sprinkle." Thus, cooks sprinkle flour with water, form a mixture, and make various pasta shapes, such as macaroni, spaghetti, and ravioli.

Pavilion

When the early French sought a term to name an area covered by a piece of cloth attached to poles, they borrowed the Latin term *papilia,* meaning "butterfly," because the flapping cloth made the structure resemble a butterfly. The French term *pavillon* gradually entered the English language as "pavilion" and came to designate a large tent or covered area.

Peaches

While the Latin noun *mala* meant specifically "apples," it was generally applied to any type of fruit. When peaches were first imported from Persia, the Romans termed this new fruit *Persica mala,* or "Persian apples." Eventually *mala* was dropped and the term *Persica* went through many changes as each succeeding generation and nation encountered the word. English derives "peaches" from the French form, *pêches.*

Peking duck

Chinese cooks used a large, white, domesticated duck as the basis for many meals. Today, we define a particular way of preparing this meal as Peking duck. The dish first became a specialty in China and is now served in gourmet restaurants around the world. It consists of a roasted duck served, according to tradition, in several courses, two of which may be strips of the meat sautéed with bean sprouts and bits of thin, crisp skin mixed with scallion and rolled in a thin pancake.

Pirogi

In the frozen food department of many supermarkets you can find boxes filled with delicious pirogi. The picture on the box shows small turnovers made of pastry crust filled with meat, cheese, mashed potatoes, or vegetables. An eastern European favorite, pirogi are aptly named since the word is the Russian plural of *pirog,* meaning "pie."

Punch

Legend traces the root of "punch" to the late 1600s. At the time, a certain drink was popular among English and other European sailors who had been visiting and exploring Indian waters. According to the earliest known recipe for the drink, it was a mixture of five ingredients: lemon, tea, sugar, water, and arrack (a strong, alcoholic drink that is usually distilled from rice, molasses, or coconut milk). Because of the strong ties between England and India, it was only natural that when the English began referring to this particularly flavorful drink as punch, all thought the name was merely an adaptation of the Hindi word *panch,* which means "five." "Punch" probably is a form of *puncheon,* the name of a large cask used for holding beer and wine aboard a ship.

Ranch

"Ranch" is a form of the Spanish American term *rancho.* Originally, *rancho* meant an area where soldiers would take their place in a line. Gradually, because of the similarity between a line of soldiers and a number of huts built one after the other, *rancho* came to denote a row of huts. The meaning changed again to represent a hut or a group of huts used by herdsmen or farm laborers out on the job. In the open expanses of America, "ranch" soon came to represent a large grazing farm with many buildings for the care and rearing of animals.

Refrigerator

The Romans called the room in the bathing complexes where patrons could take a cold bath a *frigidarium,* a word that traced its roots first to *frigerare* and then to *frigus* ("cold"). English then combined *frigerare* with the Latin preposition *re* ("again") and formed "refrigerator," the name of the appliance that keeps food cold and fresh.

The first commercial refrigerator (or "icebox") is credited to U.S. inventor Alexander C. Twining in 1856.

Sack

The Egyptians derived their noun *sak,* ("a receptacle") from their verb *sok,* meaning "to gather" or "to collect." The Greeks later adapted *sak* to *sakkos,* which the Romans changed to *saccus.* Despite the modifications in spelling, the definition changed little through the centuries.

Samovar

A combination of the Russian words *samo,* meaning "self," and *varit,* meaning "to boil," a samovar is a type of metal urn that is widely used in Russia to make tea. Usually made of brass and with a distinctive shape, a samovar has a spigot and an internal tube to heat the water within. Often there is a special place on the top of a samovar for a smaller filled teapot to sit while the tea within steeps.

Russia, the world's largest country and home to the world's largest lake (Baikal), is a federation that reaches from eastern Europe to eastern Asia. A federation is a union of states that have agreed to follow a central authority in common affairs. The country's official language is Russian (although dozens of others are spoken), and the population is approximately 150 million.

Sandwich

Tradition has it that an English gentleman named John Montagu, the fourth earl of Sandwich (1718–1792), enjoyed gambling so much that he refused to leave the gaming table to eat. Instead, he asked that his cook send him some roast beef between two slices of bread. The idea caught on, and the concoction was nicknamed the "sandwich" in his honor. Montagu also had a keen interest in naval affairs. To honor the earl's commitment to the sea, world explorer Captain James Cook named a group of islands in the Pacific Ocean the Sandwich Islands (present-day Hawaii).

Captain James Cook discovered another set of islands off the southern tip of South America in the Atlantic Ocean and also named them after the earl of Sandwich. Today they are known as the South Sandwich Islands and belong to Great Britain. These volcanic islands are covered by glaciers and were uninhabited until 1976 when Argentina tried to seize them from Britain.

Shampoo

Many English travelers to India in the 1600s observed the Indian custom of having servants use their knuckles to squeeze and knead the bodies of their masters after a hot bath. The Indian term for this practice was *champo*. Although hesitant at first, the English soon employed servants to do the same to them. Soon, a "shampoo," as the English called it, became a daily ritual. Back in England, few people could afford the luxury of having servants who gave this type of shampoo. The English modified the meaning a bit and used it to name the process of giving one's scalp and head a washing and rubbing.

Sherbet

Centuries ago, "sherbet" was coined in Asia to refer to a cold drink made by mixing together fruit juice, water, and sugar. The Turks also enjoyed the drink and adopted the word. In the 17th century, the English acquired a taste for the drink. In the United States, we now use the term to refer to a mixture of juice, sugar, and water (or milk) that has been frozen.

During a multicourse meal at some restaurants, waiters serve patrons a small dish of sherbet between two of the courses. It is used to cleanse the palate—that is, to get the taste of the last course out of your mouth so that you may better experience the next course.

Sushi

"Sushi" is a Japanese word that refers to small cakes of cooked, cold rice that have been flavored with vinegar and are served with strips of raw fish or cooked pieces of fish, egg, and vegetables.

Syrup

The Arabic noun *sharab* means "a drink" or "a beverage." "Syrup" traces its origin to that word by way of Arabic, medieval Latin, and Old French, where it referred to the juice of a fruit or plant. Today it most often describes a thick and sweet liquid made from the sap of maple trees.

People have enjoyed syrup through time. The first store brand, Log Cabin syrup, hit the market in 1887.

Tablet

"Tablet" traces its roots to *tabula,* the Latin noun for a plank or board. Centuries ago, the French adapted *tabula* to *tablete* and used it to mean a small board. English later changed the word to "tablet" to describe a flat, thin piece of wood or other material that was shaped for a specific purpose, such as a memorial or a writing pad.

Tempura

Like sushi, the Japanese word *tempura* refers to food. Tempura is a Japanese specialty that consists of pieces of vegetables, meat, fish, or fruit that have been dipped in an egg batter and then deep-fried.

Vodka

"Vodka" is a form of the Russian noun *voda,* meaning "water." Therefore, vodka translates literally into English as "little water." Vodka is an alcoholic drink made from grain.

Spectacular Sports

In the arena of sports, you can be an "amateur" or a
"professional." Either way, discovering the roots of game-
and sports-related words, such as "checkmate," "muscle,"
and "lacrosse," will expand that "little chukker" in your
head—your brain!

Amateur

An amateur is someone who participates in sports, the arts, or sciences for the pleasure of it rather than for money. The word is derived from the Latin verb *amare*, meaning "to love."

Archery/Archer

"Archery" and "archer" are both derived from the Latin noun *arcus*, meaning "bow."

Arena

The Romans called the area of the amphitheater where the gladiators fought the *harena*. The term *harena* is Latin for the word "sand." This area constantly was being covered with sand to absorb the blood of the wounded and dying gladiators. No arena does this today, and old-fashioned butcher stores, with their sawdust-sprinkled floors, may be the only ones to continue this practice.

The Colosseum in Rome is one of the more renowned amphitheaters in the world. Begun about the year 72 by the emperor Vespasian, the arena was opened by the emperor Titus and inaugurated in the year 80. It seated approximately 50,000 people and hosted many gladiatorial contests.

Camp

"Camp" can be used as a noun to refer to a military site, a summer retreat, an outdoor recreation center, or a tent or cabin set up as temporary lodging. As a verb, it means "to set up temporary living quarters." English borrowed the term from the Latin noun *campus,* meaning "field" or "level ground."

Camp David is a presidential retreat in Maryland and has been the setting for many peace talks and political negotiations.

Checkmate

Since the game of chess originated somewhere in Asia, it is fitting that the English chess term "checkmate" traces its origin to an Eastern language. In chess, when a player corners an opponent's king, the player calls "checkmate" and wins the game. The term is a form of the Persian phrase *shah mat,* which means "the king dies." To warn an opponent that his or her king is in danger, a player uses the simple word "check," from the Persian word for king.

Chess was first played in India. It spread to the Middle East around the 6th century and then to Europe by the 13th century.

Chukker

The game of polo came to England and the Western world by way of India. To play the game, players on horseback use mallets to hit a small wooden ball. Two teams compete, and the object is to drive the ball through the opponent's goal. Before a game, organizers decide whether there will be four, six, or eight periods of play. Each period is called a chukker, from the Hindi word *chukkar,* which means "a wheel" or "a circular running track for exercising horses."

Gymnastics

The Greeks greatly admired the beauty of the human body, especially as it performed on the racetrack or in athletic com-petition. The Greeks also believed that the body needed to be free of clothes to perform at its best. For many centuries, Greek men and boys trained and competed in the nude. Some histori-ans believe that this rule of no clothes helped officials enforce the law preventing women from participating in the Olympics. Also, the renowned Greek physician Hippocrates believed that the body's skin and nervous system needed direct sunlight. Thus, the Greeks formed their verb *gymnazein,* meaning "to train" or "to exercise in the nude," from their adjective *gymnos,* ("naked"). *Gymnasion* was the name given to the place where the training took place.

Judo/Jujitsu

In the 17th century, a type of fighting called *jujitsu* was favored by Japan's samurai warriors. *Jujitsu,* which uses hands and as few weapons as possible, was considered a complement to a samurai's skill as a swordsman. With the fall of the samurai in the late 19th century, *jujitsu's* popularity declined. However, many of its moves were incorporated into the fighting style known as judo. Both terms, "judo" and "jujitsu," trace their origin to the Chinese word *ju,* meaning "gentle" (in the sense that a competitor yields to his opponent's attack while at the same time trying to control it).

Samurai were the warrior class of feudal Japan that emerged in the 10th century. Their special legal position was abolished in 1868, but their influence on the government, the police, and the army continued until World War II.

Kung fu

Translated as "skill" in English, kung fu is a Chinese martial art consisting of unarmed personal combat. While there are hundreds of styles of kung fu, the moves are mostly circular and require much concentration, self-discipline, and muscle coordination.

Lacrosse

A popular sport, lacrosse involves two teams of 10 men or 12 women each. Using long-handled, pouched rackets for throwing and catching, each team tries to advance a small, hard, rubber ball across the field into the opponent's goal. The game was first played by American Indians, whose teams sometimes consisted of hundreds on each side. In the early 18th century, French missionaries and settlers saw the Algonquin Indians playing this game and called it *baggataway*. Because the webbed sticks resembled the staff of a bishop (a high-ranking Christian clergyman), the French called it *jeu de la crosse,* or "game of the crosier." A crosier is a staff with a crook at the top that is carried by a Christian bishop. In time, the phrase was shortened to "lacrosse."

Major league lacrosse began in the United States in February 1999. The professional league consists of six teams. Before 1999, only indoor, or box, lacrosse was played at the professional level in America.

Mahjong

For centuries, the Chinese have enjoyed *mahjong,* which is essentially a game of dominoes. The players use 144 pieces known as tiles made of ivory, bone, bamboo, wood, or plastic. "Mahjong" is a combination of the regional forms of two Chinese words: *mah,* meaning "the hemp plant," and *jong,* meaning "sparrow." Some people believe that the game's name refers to the noise the tiles make as the players move them on the board, a noise that is similar to the rustling of the leaves of the hemp plant or a sparrow's chirping.

Mahjong took America by storm in the 1920s, when mahjong parties became a craze.

Muscle

Flex your arm and watch the movement of the muscle. Can you see something underneath your skin that seems to run up and down along your bone? To the Romans, this looked like a little mouse. Therefore, the term *musculus,* meaning "little mouse," became associated with that particular part of the body.

Rebus

Today, "rebus" refers to a word game in which pictures of objects suggest words or phrases. For example, a picture of a key and a board would be a rebus for "keyboard." "Rebus" is both a Latin word meaning "by things" and the abbreviated form of the Latin phrase *rebus non verbis,* "by things, not words."

Regatta

Originally a Venetian term used to denote a race between gondolas, "regatta" came into the English language as a word that meant a boat race of any kind or a series of such races. "Regatta" traces its roots to the Italian verb *rigattare,* meaning "to compete."

 **The Italian city of Venice is built on 118 islands, separated by narrow canals and joined in the middle by a causeway.**

Sports

This commonly used term traces it roots to the Latin prefix *dis,* meaning "away," and the Latin verb *portare,* meaning "to carry." Technically, therefore, sports should help you relax and turn your mind away from work and problems. The word **disport**, meaning "to play," also shares the same root words.

The first issue of *Sports Illustrated* was published on August 16, 1954. The magazine's first sportsman of the year was Englishman Roger Bannister. On May 6, 1954, Bannister was the first athlete to run a mile in less than 4 minutes. His time was 3 minutes, 59.4 seconds.

Stadium

One of the major sporting events in ancient Greece was the footrace. It was also the most eagerly awaited event in the Olympic Games. The length of the standard footrace was about 600 feet, a unit of measure known to the Greeks as a *stadion.* The area designated as the course for games was one *stadion* in length and allowed runners a straight course. On the sides and ends were tiered seats for spectators. The Greeks called the space and building the *stadion,* from which the Romans derived their *stadium.* English later borrowed the Latin term intact.

The first elliptically-shaped stadium was built at Yale University in New Haven, Connecticut, in 1914. It still hosts football games today.

Taijiquan

Taijiquan is a form of boxing or gymnastics combining slow movements and breath control. It was developed by the ancient Chinese both as an exercise and as a method of attack and defense. Considered a martial art, taijiquan (better known as "tai chi") means "the grand ultimate fist" and may be practiced with or without weapons.

123

Tournament

Jousting, a fight between two knights on horseback who hold lances, was popular in Europe around 1400. When the early French sought a name for this sporting event, they noted how the knights mounted their horses and rode toward each other with their lances extended, each with the goal of knocking his opponent from his horse. The French verb *torneier,* meaning "to turn," seemed the perfect base word, since knights often rode away from each other at first and then turned and charged. From *torneier,* the noun *torneiement,* was formed, the root of "tournament."

Umpire

Sometime during the Middle Ages, the English began using the word *noumper,* meaning "an individual who did not belong to any team in a sporting event." *Noumper* was actually a combination of the Latin adverb *non,* meaning "not," and the Latin adjective *par,* meaning "equal." Through the years, *noumper* was incorrectly pronounced and became "umpire."

Joyful Journeys

Whether you prefer a "cruise" or a "safari," or measure
your "journey" in "knots" or "milestones," this chapter
offers a few words to guide you on your "adventure"
of discovering the roots of travel words.

Adventure

This noun has come to mean action a bit more exciting than its root words suggest. "Adventure" is a combination of the Latin preposition *ad,* meaning "to," and the Latin verb *venire,* meaning "to come." In English, an adventure usually is an experience that involves daring and danger.

Caravan

A caravan is a group of travelers or vehicles journeying together. The word has changed little from the definition of its root word, the Persian noun *karwan,* which means "a company of individuals traveling together for safety."

Carry-all

A carry-all is a convenient bag that holds whatever you need for a short trip. Its origin is the French noun *carriole,* meaning "a light, covered, one-horse carriage that seats several people."

Cruise

Following the Age of Exploration in the 15th and 16th centuries, the Dutch, English, Portuguese, and Spanish became great trade rivals, each importing and exporting goods around the world. Some captains and sailors became pirates because they found it more profitable to seize another ship's cargo than to transport their own. Pirate ships had no set schedule or course. Rather they crossed and crisscrossed the oceans, seeking victims. The Dutch called this type of sailing *kruisen,* from their word *kruis,* meaning "cross." *Kruis,* in turn, traces its roots to the Latin noun *crux,* which also means "cross." In the 17th century, the English borrowed the term, adapted it to "cruise," and used it to refer to warships crossing the waters in search of the enemy. In time, speakers of English used it to refer to pleasure boats crossing the water, but with no purpose or timetable. Today, "cruise" refers to any type of pleasure trip on a boat.

Journey/Journal

"Journey" originally referred to the distance a person covered in a day's march, while "journal" referred to the events that occurred in one day. Both trace their roots to the Latin adjective *diurnum,* meaning "daily."

Homer's *Odyssey* recounts the long journey home of the Greek hero Odysseus. This work is one of the world's best and most famous examples of epic poetry.

Knot

A knot measures a ship's speed at sea, or how many nautical miles the ship travels in an hour. For centuries, sailors measured a ship's speed using a log line, a rope divided by knots every 50 feet. Sailors tied a log to the end of the rope, threw it overboard, and then counted the number of knots that moved past a checkpoint in half a minute. If 10 knots went by, they were moving at a speed of 10 knots, or roughly 10 nautical miles per hour. One nautical mile is 796 feet longer than a land-measured mile, which is 5,280 feet.

Map

During the Middle Ages, European mapmakers drew their charts on cloth because it was considered a durable material. Since Latin was the most widely used language at the time in Europe, it was common to use the Latin word *mappa,* meaning "cloth," for the material the cartographers used. Gradually, *mappa* came to refer specifically to geographical drawings. English later shortened it to "map."

The Greeks credited the philosopher Anaximander of Miletus as the first mapmaker.

Milestone

In the early days of the Roman Empire, a large stone was positioned in the Forum at Rome. Along the roads leading out of Rome were additional markers. Each represented a distance of 1,000 paces. (One pace equals approximately five feet. So 1,000 paces would be the equivalent of one mile.) Chiseled on each stone was the distance from Rome to the site of the stone. Such a stone was called a *milliarium,* from the Latin term *mille,* meaning "thousand." Our **mile** is a derivative of *mille.*

Forums were marketing and meeting places in ancient Roman towns. In ancient Rome, the Forum was centrally located in the valley between the Capitoline and Palatine hills. It was here that, in 20 B.C., the Roman emperor Augustus set up a Golden Milestone, a marble column with gilt-bronze plates. *See also* palace (*page 110*).

Route

This often-used word, which refers to a road, highway, or regularly traveled path, has an interesting history. The Romans referred to a pathway that had been cleared for travel as a *via rupta,* meaning "a road having been broken." The French adapted the Latin participle *ruptus* ("having been broken") to *route.* The English adopted the French word and its meaning with no changes. Other English words that trace their origins to *rupta* are: **routine** ("a behavior pattern that is followed regularly"), **rote** ("a mechanical way of doing the same thing repeatedly"), and **rout** ("a disorderly retreat, usually by military forces").

Safari

Originally "safari" was used to describe a great hunting expedition, especially into the jungles of Africa. The word is used today to refer to any travel expedition that involves adventure. This change brings "safari" closer to its origin, the Arabic word *safara,* meaning "travel."

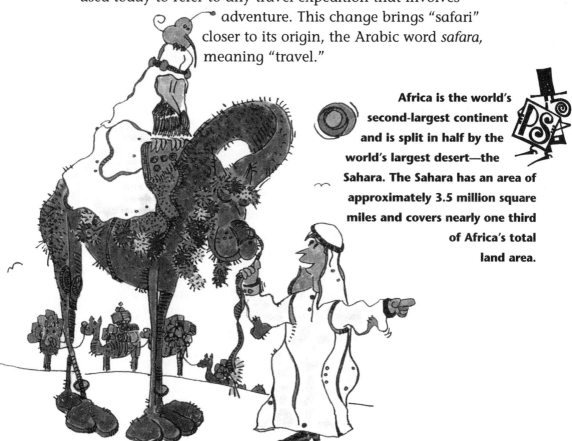

Africa is the world's second-largest continent and is split in half by the world's largest desert—the Sahara. The Sahara has an area of approximately 3.5 million square miles and covers nearly one third of Africa's total land area.

Joyful Journeys

Sampan

A combination of the Chinese word *sam,* meaning "three," and *pan,* meaning "plank," a sampan is a small boat used in China and Japan that is rowed with an oar in the stern. Some sampans have a sail and a small cabin made of mats.

Starboard

Centuries ago, sailors steered their boats by working a large oar on the right side of the vessel. To name this side of a ship, the early English used *steorbord,* (later "starboard") meaning "steer side." When loading or unloading supplies, sailors naturally used the left side of the vessel, where there was no oar to interfere with their work. The English called the left side the *ladebord* (later *larboard*) or "loading side." Because the names were so similar, accidents did happen when someone mistook larboard for starboard. To simplify matters, "port" was substituted for larboard since the left side of a boat was the one closest to the dock or port. Today, "starboard" refers to the right side and "port" refers to the left side of any boat. *See also* **port** *(page 26).*

Travel/Travail

Would you ever guess that "travel" and "travail" both trace their roots to the Latin words *tres* and *palus,* meaning "three" and "stick"? In the Middle Ages, the French used an instrument to torture people that was composed of three pieces of wood. To name this device, the French borrowed the two Latin words and formed *trepalium.* As the years passed, the French modified *trepalium* to *travailler* and used it as a verb meaning "to work hard." English borrowed *travailler,* changed the spelling to "travail" but left the meaning the same. "Travail" also came to mean "going from one place to another." Journeys at this time were quite difficult—roads were not paved and the threat of an attack by bandits or wild beasts was always a possibility. Gradually, two English words developed: "travail," meaning "hard work," and "travel," meaning "a journey."

Voyage

The Latin term for road or passage is *via.* To designate the provisions one needed for a journey of some distance, the Romans used *via* as a base and formed *viaticum.* The Italians borrowed the term, but changed both the spelling and the meaning. The Italian *viaggio* means "the trip" rather than "the necessities for the trip." The English language later adapted *viaggio* to "voyage."

Natural Necessities

From "canary" to "ibis" to "pigeon," this chapter
on the natural world reveals that birds who are *not*
of a feather can still flock together—when it comes to
tracing their word origins.

Aviator/Aviary

Both words are derived from *avis,* the Latin term for bird. Since the person who operates an airplane is similar to a bird using its wings, "aviator" became a synonym for pilot. When a word was sought to describe a place for keeping birds, it was decided to modify the Latin term *avis,* and "aviary" was formed.

Balsa

In the 16th century, Spanish sailors off the coast of South America noticed how well the rafts used by the natives floated. They sat high on the surface, unlike their own that settled into the water when any weight was put on board. To name the tree logs that the natives lashed together with vines to make their rafts, the Spanish used their noun *balsa,* meaning "raft" or "float." Today, "balsa" still refers to the tropical American tree with extremely light but strong wood.

For a good example of balsa, go to your local toy store. Many toy planes are made of this lightweight wood.

Biology

Biology is the study of plants and animals. The prefix "bio" is derived from the Greek noun *bios,* meaning "life," while the Greek noun *logos,* means "word," "thought," or "statement."

Bonsai

This term means "tray-planted" and designates dwarf trees and the art of growing and training these trees in containers. Although the art of bonsai originated in China centuries ago, the Japanese are the leaders in the field today.

Canary

When the ancient Romans first landed on what is now called the Canary Islands, they were amazed at the number of wild dogs roaming the islands. They used their term *canaries,* "relating to a dog," to name the islands the *Canaria Insula.* (*Insula* is the Latin word for "island.") Later, when ornithologists were deciding what to name the little yellow finches that were native to these islands, they used the name of their homeland as the root. Thus, the term "canary" was created.

Ebony

The tree that produced the hard black ebony wood that was so highly prized in Egypt and the ancient Mediterranean world is technically called *dalbergia melanoxylon.* It was not native to Egypt but imported from the lands to the south. The Egyptian word for wood, *hbny,* was adapted in Hebrew to *habnim* and in Greek to *ebenos.* Although "ebony" definitely used the Greek term as its root, further study may prove that *hbny* may have come from a language used further south of Egypt.

Geyser

Hot springs are a natural phenomenon in Iceland, where in an area of approximately two square miles about 100 hot springs pour forth from the ground. To name a hot spring that throws out jets of water, the Icelandic people used their term *geysa,* meaning "to rush furiously," and formed the word *geysir,* the root of our English word.

The world's first permanent parliament (the Althing) was established in Iceland in the year 930. Many countries have a form of parliament, an assembly whose responsibilities include making laws.

Gladiolus/Gladiator

Next time you see a bunch of gladioluses, look closely at the long, sword-shaped spikes of the flowers and at the leaves. They resemble the short little sword used by gladiators, and their shape gave the plant its name. The ancient Romans used their noun for "sword," *gladius,* as the base for the flower's name. They inserted the letters "ol," which were used to mean "small," and formed *gladiolus.*

Gladiatorial combat was first introduced to Rome in 264 B.C. In the decades that followed, prisoners of war, slaves, and condemned criminals were trained to fight one another in public arenas. They became known as gladiators, which in Latin literally means "one who uses a sword."

Gum

The acadia tree is known by its clusters of yellow or white flowers. Also characteristic of several varieties found in Egypt is a substance found within the bark that has a sticky, fluid consistency. This gummy substance, which the ancient Egyptians called *kmyt,* was used chiefly as incense and glue in the mummification process. By the fifth century B.C., Greeks visiting and trading in Egypt who knew and used *kymt* had adapted the Egyptian term to *kommi.* The changes continued through the centuries. The Romans spelled it *gummi,* and the French later adapted it to *gomme.* Gradually, "gum" came to refer to the gummy substances, known also as resins, that are found in trees and shrubs beyond Egypt's borders.

ibis

The ibis is a large wading bird found mainly in tropical regions. It has long legs and a long, slender, curved bill. The Egyptians used the term *hb* to refer to this stork-like bird, which they considered sacred to Thoth, their god of reading, writing, and learning. How they pronounced this term is not exactly known, since they wrote using only consonant sounds. Many Egyptologists and etymologists believe that *hb* was pronounced "hibey."

The first Egyptian pharaoh to be buried in the Valley of the Kings was Thutmose I (active 1524–1518 B.C.)

Jade

In China, jade is known as *yu*, "fairest of stones." It is one of the country's most treasured materials. The Western version of jade is much less dramtic and probably originated with the Spanish conquest of the New World in the 16th century. When the Spaniards first discovered jade in the Yucatan Peninsula of Central America, they called it *piedra de ijada*, meaning "stone of the side," because it was believed that it could heal the pain in one's side. The term *ijada* was later adapted to "jade" by French and English speakers. In the West, jade came to describe the apple-green color characteristic of jadeite, a rock that has never been found in China. The main type of jade used by the Chinese, especially during the Han dynasty, was nephrite, whose colors range from deep, greenish black to pale, greenish white.

According to history, for centuries the Chinese believed that jade could prevent decay. Some even thought that jade could help them live forever. They distilled it in liquid and drank it.

Jungle

In Sanskrit, the term *jangala* was used to describe dry desert land. As various languages based on Sanskrit developed, *jangala* continued to be used, but more in reference to land areas that could not be cultivated. In the late 19th and early 20th centuries, when India was part of the British Empire, the British began to use *jangala* to refer to the lush forest of India. Although this use seems the exact opposite of the word's original meaning, it is important to remember that neither type of land can be cultivated, one because of dry soil and the other because of thick growth. English gradually adapted *jangala* to "jungle."

India is currently the world's seventh-largest country and the second most populous. India is also home to one of the world's oldest civilizations, which originally began in the Indus Valley.

Lilac

In ancient Sanskrit, the term *nila* means "to appear very dark." *Nila* entered the Persian language as *nilak,* meaning "bluish." The Arabs later adopted the term, changing it to *laylak.* At some point, *laylak* came to be associated with a flowering plant. When the Spanish introduced this plant to England sometime in the 17th century, it arrived with the name "lilac," a term that now refers to both the plant and its color.

Mistletoe

For centuries, mistletoe was considered a sacred plant because it flourished on bare-branched trees throughout the winter. Most etymologists agree that the "toe" of "mistletoe" traces its roots to the Anglo-Saxon term *tan,* meaning "twig." The origin of "mistle" is not so easy to trace. In Old English, *mistel* means "fog" or "mist," but many believe that the German *mist,* which means "dung," is the root word because tradition says that this plant grew from bird droppings.

Oasis

An oasis is a fertile place in the desert. The ancient Greeks recognized this and used the word to mean just that. Etymologists believe that "oasis" traces its roots to the Egyptian noun *wahet*, meaning a "caldron" or "large kettle." Just as a caldron is a deep pot, so an oasis is a deep impression in the desert.

Parsley

In ancient Greece, the victors in athletic contests were crowned with wreaths of leaves. For certain events, a garland of parsley was awarded the victor. The Greek word for parsley was *petroselinon*. However, as the centuries passed and other languages began to add foreign terms into their vocabularies, the original Greek form became *peresil* in French, from which came our "parsley."

According to an old English proverb, "Parsley grows for the wicked, but not for the just." The ancient Romans believed that eating parsley allowed a person to drink without becoming drunk.

Peat

Peat is a partially decayed, moisture-absorbing plant matter that is found in ancient bogs and swamps. It is used for fuel and to cover and protect plants. The term most likely traces its roots first to the medieval Latin form *peta*, which was probably used to denote a "piece of land." *Peta*, in turn, probably derives from the Celtic *pett*, meaning "piece."

Natural Necessities

Pekingese

The Pekingese breed of dog traces it roots to China. "Peking" is a western term used in the past to represent Beijing, the capital of China. A Pekingese dog is easily recognizable with its pug nose, protruding eyes, small body, short legs, and long silky hair.

Pelican

It is believed that the Greek philosopher Aristotle first used the term *pelekan* when referring to a woodpecker. Since *pelekan* is a derivative of the Greek word *pelekos,* meaning "ax," it is thought the name was used to designate a bird with an interesting beak. In time, however, the term was used to represent not the woodpecker, but the pelican, whose beak formation is even more extraordinary.

Pheasant

Since this bird came from an area near the river Phasis (today's Rion), which flows into the Black Sea, the Greeks named it *phaisianos.* English ornithologists merely adapted the term and formed "pheasant."

Pigeon

This name traces its origin back through Middle English to the Old French term *pyjoun,* which meant "a young bird," especially a young dove. *Pyjoun* was, in turn, a derivative of the late Latin term *pipionem,* "a chirping bird." The original Latin form had been *pipiare,* a verb the Romans used to represent the peeping and chirping of a young bird.

Plover

The name of this bird traces its history through the Old French term *plover* to the Latin term *pluvial,* meaning "rain." Some say *pluvia* was used as the base because the spotty upper feathers of the bird remind one of rain or of something in the rain. Etymologists do not agree, and no definitive reason for its name has been given.

Ruminate

"Ruminate" describes how an animal chews its food, swallows it into its first stomach, brings it up through its throat, and chews it again more thoroughly. When we see cows doing this, we say they are chewing their cud, or ruminating, from the Latin term *rumen,* meaning "throat." "Ruminate" also describes the thought process when humans reconsider action or ideas a second or third time.

Saffron

Saffron is made from a species of crocus that has purple flowers. Since approximately 40,000 blossoms are needed to make an ounce of saffron, it is one of the world's most expensive spices. English adapted the Old French spelling of the spice, *safran,* which, in turn, traced its roots through the medieval Latin term *safranum* to the Arabic name for the spice, *za'faran.*

Saffron is native to Asia Minor, a peninsula in west Asia that makes up most of what is present-day Turkey.

Steppe

Steppe, from the Russian *styep',* refers to the broad expanse of grassland, broken up in some areas by mountains. The Russian steppe extends from Hungary eastward across the Ukraine and southern Russia into central Asia and Manchuria.

Typhoon

A violent, cyclone-type storm originating in the west Pacific, especially in the South China Sea, is known as a typhoon. The name traces its roots to the Chinese phrase *taifeng,* meaning "great wind."

Volcano

The ancient Greeks and Romans worshiped many gods. One was Vulcan, the son of Jupiter, king of the Roman gods. A skilled workman and the patron of all artisans, Vulcan was usually pictured in his workshop with his anvil and forge. No one knew the exact location of the shop, but the Romans believed it must have been located wherever fire burst forth from within the earth's crust. Therefore, whenever an eruption or an earthquake did occur, the Romans said Vulcan must have been at work in his shop. When later generations sought a word to designate the area from which molten rock, hot steam, and ash spewed forth, they appropriately chose the name *Vulcanus* (Vulcan's name in Latin) and converted it to "volcano."

Awesome Archaeology

You will see a number of words in this chapter that
have the root word "-ology." This root is derived from the
Greek noun *logos,* which means "word," "thought" or
"statement." Just to give you a jump-start, these "-ology"
words usually mean "the study of" something
relating to people and cultures.

Acropolis

At least one out of every 10 English words traces it roots to an ancient Greek term. Take, for example, the Greek noun *polis,* which means "city." By adding Greek prefixes, English acquired several words, each with its own distinct meaning. "Acropolis" (from the Greek *akros* —"highest"—and *polis*—"city") is an upper, fortified part of a Greek city. *See also* **metropolis** *(page 159) and* **necropolis** *(page 160).*

Ancestor

The ancient Romans often used Latin past participles as the base for other words, adding a variety of prefixes to form words with related meanings. For example, to *cessus* (meaning "gone"), they added *ante* ("before"), *pro* ("forward"), and *re* ("back"). In time, *antecessus* gave us "ancestor," or "one who goes before." *Processus* became **procession** ("moving along or forward"), and *recessus* evolved to **recession** ("withdrawing or going back").

Archaeology

Archaeology is the study of the life and culture of past people, especially ancient peoples. The prefix is derived from the Greek adjective *archaios,* meaning "old" or "ancient," and the Greek noun *logos,* meaning "word," "thought," or "statement."

Artifact

An artifact is any object, weapon, or tool that has been fashioned by humans. "Artifact" is actually just a translation of its Latin roots *arte* ("by skill") and *factum* ("made").

Dendrochronology

Dendrochronology, the technique of using tree rings to date wooden artifacts uncovered at excavation sites, is an archaeological technique used throughout the world. The term is a compound of several Greek words: *dendron,* meaning "tree"; *chronos,* meaning "time"; and *logos,* meaning "word," "thought," or "statement."

Etymology/Etymologist

Etymos is the Greek adjective for "true" and *logos* is the Greek noun for "word." English combined these two words to form "etymology," which means "the history of terms" or the development of a word from its earliest beginnings to its present form and usage. An etymologist is a person who studies the origin and development of words.

Excavate

The Latin preposition *ex* means "out of" and the Latin verb *cavare* means "to make hollow." So, when archaeologists excavate, they are doing exactly as the word implies.

Fossil

The ancient Romans thought it quite appropriate to use the verbal participle *fossus* ("dug up") to form the noun *fossa* ("ditch"). Centuries later, English borrowed *fossa*, changed it to "fossil," and used it to refer to anything that was dug up out of the ground. In time, the meaning narrowed, and today a fossil refers to the hardened remains of ancient plant or animal life.

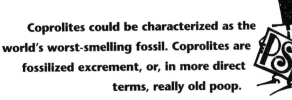

Coprolites could be characterized as the world's worst-smelling fossil. Coprolites are fossilized excrement, or, in more direct terms, really old poop.

Hieroglyphs

As early as 2600 B.C., the Egyptians had developed a well-organized system of writing. When the Greeks discovered these mysterious images carved into stone centuries later, they combined their words *hieros,* meaning "sacred," and *glyphein,* meaning "to carve." This formed the term *hieroglyphikos.*
The Romans adopted the Greek term, for they, too, could not solve the riddle of the pictures. In fact, as many other nations introduced the ancient Greek term into vocabulary, the term "hieroglyphs" gradually came to signify any symbol, sign, or writing that is difficult to read or understand. In 1799, near Rosetta, Egypt, a black basalt stone was discovered by Napoleon's troops. Inscribed on it, the so-called Rosetta Stone, was a decree in honor of the Egyptian king Ptolemy V, who ruled from about 204 to 181 B.C. Since the priests wished everyone to understand their edict, it was written in three languages: hieroglyphs, demotic (a later form of Egyptian writing), and Greek. By comparing and contrasting the known forms with the unknown, language experts were finally able to decipher the ancient Egyptian symbols. After the mystery was solved and it was learned that every picture did not represent a sacred carving, the term "hieroglyphs" continued to be used to represent the written language of the early Egyptians.

British doctor Thomas Young was the first to make major steps in deciphering the mysterious Rosetta Stone. He published his findings in 1819. Egyptologist Jean-François Champollion completely translated the Rosetta Stone in 1822.

Mausoleum

When Mausolus, king of Caria in southwestern Asia Minor (present-day Turkey), died in 353 B.C., his wife, Artemesia, was so upset that she resolved to build a fitting memorial to her husband. After performing the traditional funeral rites, she ordered a grand tomb built in the Carian city of Halicarnassus. The Latin form of the name for this type of building, *mausoleum,* continues to be used today to refer to any grand burial structure.

The mausoleum at Halicarnassus was considered one of the seven wonders of the ancient world. In the 1300s, after standing for almost 1,800 years, it crumbled during an earthquake.

Medieval

"Medieval" refers to the Middle Ages and anything characteristic of this historical period. It traditionally includes the years between 476 and 1453, which roughly date from the fall of Rome to the broadening of the Renaissance. It is a combination of two Latin words that mean "middle age"—the adjective *medius,* and the noun *aevum.*

Megalith

"Megalith" traces its origin to *lithos,* Greek for "stone." English added a variety of Greek prefixes to form words that refer to a specific type of stone or to people who work with stone. Thus, "megalith" (*megas* means "great") denotes "a huge stone." **Monolith** (*monos* means "single") denotes "a single, large stone block." **Neolithic** (*neos* means "new") refers to that ancient time period when people first used polished stone tools. "Megalith" refers especially to large standing stones that people in the Neolithic period used to construct monuments by arranging them in circles and rows. The best-known megalith is found at Stonehenge in England.

Obelisk

Called *tekhenu* by the Egyptians, obelisks are tall columns carved from a single piece of stone. The four sides of an obelisk narrow toward the top and end in a point. The Egyptians believed obelisks were sacred to the sun and to the solar gods. The ancient Greeks called them *obeliskos,* meaning "small spits," such as those used

 for roasting meat. Centuries later, English and other languages adapted the Greek form. Many travelers arranged to have obelisks sent back to their countries. Today, Egyptians obelisks can be found in Rome, London, Paris, Istanbul, and New York. In the late 19th century, Egypt presented the United States with the obelisk that currently stands in New York City's Central Park. Dating to about 1500 B.C., this obelisk originally was erected by the New Kingdom pharaoh Thutmose III.

An obelisk had to be carved from a single block of stone with no imperfections that would cause it to split when it was being shaped.

Paleoanthropology

This term refers to the study of the fossil record of early humans. The prefix "pale" is derived from the Greek adjective *palaios,* meaning "ancient." The base word *anthropo* is actually the Greek noun *anthropos,* meaning "man" or "human being." *Logos* is the Greek noun for "word," "thought," or "statement."

Paleontology

The study of life on earth in ancient times, particularly through surviving fossil remains is known as paleontology. "Pale" comes from the Greek *palaios,* meaning "ancient," and "onto" comes from the Greek *onta* meaning "existing." Finally, *logos* is the Greek noun meaning "word," "thought," or "statement."

Pyramid

Ancient Greek scholars loved to travel and study in Egypt. The massive royal tombs built along the desert's edge fascinated them. Some sources suggest that the Greeks adapted the Egyptian word *puramides* to their term *pyramis*, which means a particular type of wheat and honey cake. The shape of the cake resembled the cone-shaped forms of the pyramids.

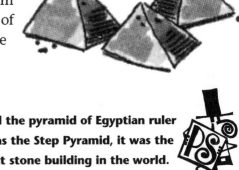

Imhotep designed the pyramid of Egyptian ruler Djoser. Known as the Step Pyramid, it was the first great stone building in the world. Imhotep's reputation as a physician also earned him the honor of being worshiped as a god of healing by the Egyptians.

Renaissance

The Renaissance was the period in European history from 1350 to 1550 when there was a rebirth of the arts and sciences based on Greek and Roman sources. The term is a combination of the Latin prefix *re*, meaning "back" or "again," and the Latin verb *nascere*, meaning "to be born." The Renaissance led Western civilization from the Middle Ages into modern times.

In the 1400s, Cosimo del Medici, the Elder, founded the first public library in Italy. He also established the Platonic Academy in Florence to promote classical and humanist ideas. In time, it helped spread the ideas of the Renaissance.

Sinologist

A sinologist is a person whose field of study is the Chinese language, literature, art, and customs. It is a combination of two Greek words, *Sinai* ("an Oriental people") and *logos* ("word," "thought," or "statement").

About half of all basic inventions used today originally came from China. They include the toothbrush, toothpaste, toilet paper, coal for heating, the stirrup, the kite, the yo-yo, gunpowder, the wheelbarrow, the umbrella, porcelain, and spaghetti.

Tradition

Traditions include stories, beliefs, and customs of a people that are handed down from generation to generation. The ancient Romans combined the Latin preposition *trans* ("across") and the Latin participle *datum* ("given") to form *tradere*, the root of "tradition."

Prince Albert, the husband of Queen Victoria, who ruled England from 1837 to 1901, introduced the German Christmas tradition of candlelit trees, surrounded with gifts, to England.

Political Powerhouse

From "civilization" to "people" to "democracy," the
English language has adopted many terms that are
important in defining ourselves and our political systems.

Alcatraz

When the Muslims ruled southern Spain, many Arabic words entered the Spanish vocabulary. From the Arabic noun *al-qadus*, meaning "water carrier," the Spanish formed two words: *arcaduz*, meaning "a bucket" or "a channel for water," and *alcatraz*, meaning "a pelican." According to the thinking at the time, the Spanish believed that pelicans used their bucket-like bills to bring water to their young, hence the coining of the term "alcatraz." Years later, the Spanish named the island in San Francisco Bay Alcatraz because it was home to a large pelican colony.

Alcatraz Island first housed a military prison in 1868. From 1934 to 1963 it served as a prison for dangerous civilian prisoners. Some of its famous residents were Al Capone, George "Machine Gun" Kelly, and Robert Stroud, the "Birdman of Alcatraz."

Alibi

This commonly used English noun is actually a Latin adverb. More than 2,000 years ago, the Romans combined *alius*, meaning "other," and *ibi*, meaning "at another place" or "elsewhere." English uses this term primarily in a legal context to refer to a witness's proof that he or she was not at the scene of a crime.

Amnesty

Tradition says that a Greek general was the first to grant an enemy amnesty. That is to say, he officially pardoned those whom he had opposed in battle and chose not to remember the acts they had committed against his country and people. In Greek, the word for this action is *amnestia*, which means "a forgetting." *Amnestia* is itself a derivative of the Greek prefix *a*, meaning "not," and the Greek verb *mnasthai*, meaning "to remember."

Anarchy

This term refers to a political situation in which there is no legitimate or commonly recognized leadership. Such a situation can involve violence and lawlessness. Fittingly, "anarchy" traces it roots to the Greek words *an,* meaning "without," and *arches,* meaning "a leader." An **anarchist** is someone who rebels against authority or an established order.

The father of the philosophy known as Stoicism, Zeno of Citium, is also known as the father of anarchism. Stoics—followers of Stoicism—believe that one achieves virtue only by living in harmony with nature.

Aristocracy

Two Greek words—*aristos,* meaning "best," and *kratos,* meaning "rule," "power," or "strength"—combine to form "aristocracy," which refers to a government of the noble class or wealthiest people. An **aristocrat** is a member of the privileged upper class and a person whose social position and wealth is usually inherited.

Assassin

In 11th-century Persia, a man referred to as the Old Man of the Mountains founded a small secret society whose members were feared throughout the Persian Empire. The main purpose of the group was to terrorize and kill leaders of the Crusades as they traveled to the Holy Land. Followers of the old man committed their crimes under the influence of the drug hashish. As a result, they became known as *hashshashin,* the Arabic term for "hashish eaters." English borrowed the name and changed it to "assassin." Today, the term is used to refer to anyone who murders a high-ranking or notable person.

The first U.S. president subject to an assassination attempt was Andrew Jackson. The first president to be assassinated was Abraham Lincoln in 1865.

Bobby

In England, the common name for a police officer is "bobby." The word traces its origin to sometime between 1828 and 1830, when British Home Secretary Sir Robert Peel reorganized the London police force. Since Peel's nickname was "Bobby," many English people began using Peel's nickname for their police officers.

Candidate

In ancient Rome, a citizen who was campaigning for public office would make sure his toga was as white as possible. The Romans began using their word *candidatus,* which means "clothed in white," to refer to candidates for public office. *Candidatus* is itself a derivative of another Latin word—the adjective *candidus,* which means "white."

City

This term traces its history to the Latin noun *civitas,* meaning "citizenship" or "community." Actually, *civitas* is a derivative of the Latin noun *civis,* meaning "citizen."

The first American city to have gas streetlights was Baltimore, Maryland. They were installed in 1817.

Civilization

Civilization refers to the process of coming from a primitive or savage condition into a social organization that is marked by the development and use of a written language and by advances in the arts, sciences, and government practices. The Latin root of this noun is simple and to the point—*civis* ("a citizen"). *Civis* was a key word in the ancient Roman vocabulary. A *civis* was a person who held the prized rights of Roman citizenship, as opposed to a foreigner (an outsider with no privileges) or an enemy. Other words that are derived from *civis* are **citizen** ("a person owing loyalty to and entitled to protection from a state or nation"), **civics** ("the branch of political science that deals with the rights and duties of citizens"), and **civil** ("relating to or characteristic of a citizen").

Curfew

During the Middle Ages, the law dictated that fires used as lights along the streets had to be extinguished when the evening bell tolled. After the French conquered England in 1066, the French phrase *couvre feu* ("cover the fire") was commonly heard in England. The English adopted the phrase and changed it to "curfew."

Democracy

"Democracy" is composed of two Greek words: *demos,* meaning "people," and *kratos,* meaning "rule" or "strength." It translates to "a government by the people." A **democrat** is someone who believes in or supports this type of government.

Dynasty

This word refers to a succession of rulers, all of whom are members of the same family. History has many examples of dynasties around the world, such as those in China, Egypt, England, and India. "Dynasty" traces it roots to the ancient Greek noun *dynamis,* meaning "power" or "force," and from the Greek verb *dynasthai,* meaning "to be strong."

The first documented dynasty in China was the Shang (about 1766 to about 1122 B.C.). The last dynasty in China was the Qing, which ended in 1911.

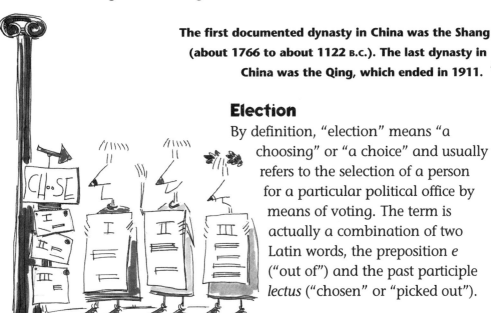

Election

By definition, "election" means "a choosing" or "a choice" and usually refers to the selection of a person for a particular political office by means of voting. The term is actually a combination of two Latin words, the preposition *e* ("out of") and the past participle *lectus* ("chosen" or "picked out").

155

Embargo

When a country wishes to express its disapproval of another country's actions, it often imposes an embargo on that country. Originally, this decree prohibited all commercial ships belonging to the country against which the embargo is in effect from leaving or entering the ports of the country imposing the embargo. Today it can refer to any prohibition of trade. The word is a derivative of the Latin prefix *in* ("in" or "on") and the medieval Latin word *barra* ("barrier").

Empire

"Empire" is one of several English words that traces it roots to the Latin verb *imperare*, meaning "to command." Others are **emperor, imperial**, and **imperious**. *Imperare* is actually a derivative of two Latin words, the preposition *in*, meaning "in," and the verb *parare*, meaning "to set in order." An emperor is a male ruler of an empire. Imperial is suggestive of an empire or having supreme authority. Someone who is imperious is arrogantly domineering or overbearing.

The British Empire was one of the largest the world has ever known. The seeds of its establishment date to the 1500s and the great era of exploration. By 1914, the British Empire included almost 25 percent of the earth's land surface and population.

Escape

In times past, men and women often wore traveling capes or cloaks. If a person was chased by someone and caught by the cloak, he or she could break free by quickly unfastening the cloak. To show this action, "escape" was formed by joining two Latin terms—the preposition *ex*, meaning "out of," and the noun *cappa*, meaning "cape."

Fascism

The Etruscans used a bundle of hollow rods bound together with red thongs to symbolize the authority of their leaders. They inserted an ax into the bundle to indicate absolute authority. The Romans continued the tradition but removed the ax within the city limits. *Fasces* is the plural of their term *fascis* ("bundle"). In the early 1900s, members of an Italian organization later headed by Benito Mussolini called themselves Fascists. As a symbol, they used the Roman *fasces* because they felt it represented their philosophy, which called for strict enforcement of law and order and intense national pride. The movement spread, and the term "fascism" came into being.

The Fascist movement (1922–1943) headed by the Italian dictator Benito Mussolini formed in response to a lack of leadership and difficult economic times following World War I. Members of the Fascist party wore black shirts, organized themselves into military groups, and used a straight, outstretched arm as their traditional greeting.

Govern

The comparison between a leader ruling a country and a captain skippering a boat is an old one. Ancient Greek texts often use the phrase "ship of state" to mean a country or city-state. When the Greeks sought a word to describe a ruler's ability to guide the country, they used their verb *kybernan,* meaning "to steer a boat." The Romans adopted the term, Latinizing it to *gubernare.* English further adapted the term to "govern." The meaning, however, has remained much the same.

Grand vizier

The Ottoman Empire was a hereditary Islamic state that controlled southeast Europe, the Middle East, and North Africa from the 14th to 20th centuries. The highest-ranking public official of the empire was the grand vizier. He was entrusted with much decision making. "Vizier" traces its roots to the Arabic term *wazier,* "the bearer of burdens."

Guillotine

A monster in the shape of a machine is what many people considered the guillotine. This 18th-century invention was used by French independence fighters to behead their captured enemies. The gruesome machine chopped off a person's head with a large blade. It was named after Joseph I. Guillotin, a doctor who suggested that such a device be used.

"Guillotine" also refers to a parliamentary device whereby a government imposes a time limit on discussions of legislation.

iron Curtain

On March 5, 1946, Winston Churchill, who had been Great Britain's prime minister during World War II, was in the United States to receive an honorary degree from Westminster College in Fulton, Missouri. In a speech, Churchill voiced his misgivings about the growing Russian influence over Eastern Europe when he said, "From Stettin in the Baltic to Trieste in the Adriatic, an iron curtain has descended across the continent." Almost immediately, Churchill's "iron curtain" phrase was adopted by other statesmen and nations to refer to Russia's insistence on isolating itself and its territories from the world.

"I have nothing to offer but blood, toil, tears, and sweat," declared Winston Churchill on becoming prime minister of England. He held the post from 1940 to 1945 and from 1951 to 1955.

Jury

The English noun "jury" is derived from the Latin verb *jurare*, meaning "to swear an oath." Today, members of a jury in a court swear an oath to uphold the law.

Libel

The Latin noun for book, *liber*, originally meant "bark." In very ancient times, the bark of certain trees was used as writing material and to make books, so *liber* soon acquired a second meaning. In later centuries, attacks against laws, individuals, and ideas were often made by writing the accusation on several sheets of paper. The authors then distributed these "little books." To name this type of defamatory accusation, English adopted the Latin term for "little book," *libellus,* and changed it to "libel."

Maharajah

A maharajah is a prince who ruled one of India's chief regions. Its origin is the Hindi adjective *maha,* meaning "great," and the Sanskrit noun *raja,* meaning "king."

Metropolis

This word is formed by combining the Greek noun *polis,* which means "city," with the Greek prefix *metro,* meaning "mother." Thus "metropolis" means "a mother or parent city, a chief city." *See also* **acropolis** *(page 144) and* **necropolis** *(page 160).*

Mob

The word "mob" is actually an abbreviation. Before 1700, when an English-speaking person wished to refer to the populace or to a disorderly group of people, he used the Latin phrase *mobile vulgus. Mobile,* which means "changeable" or "fickle," modified the noun *vulgus,* meaning "the populace" or "a crowd." Early in the 18th century, this phrase seemed too lengthy to some and it was shortened to "mob."

Monarchy

Referring to a government ruled by a king or queen, "monarchy" is formed from the Greek words *mono,* meaning "alone" and *arches,* meaning "a leader." A **monarch** is the sole ruler of a state or country.

Necropolis

By combining the Greek noun *polis,* which means "city," with *nekros,* meaning "a dead body," English has "necropolis," which describes a cemetery.

Ninja

This is a Japanese word meaning "hired assassin." In Japanese, *nin* means "to endure" and *ja* means "person." The samurai (formerly, members of Japan's military class) often employed the ninja, who dressed completely in black for nighttime work and in khaki for daytime assignments. Since the ninja belonged to a secret society, there are few written records concerning their organization.

Oligarchy

From a combination of the Greek words *oligos,* meaning "a few," and *arches,* meaning "a leader," we get "oligarchy," which refers to a government ruled by a few individuals. An **oligarch** is a member of a small government faction.

Ostracize

In ancient Athens, if the people wished to banish a particular person from the city, a special meeting of the Assembly (adult male citizens) was called. If 6,000 votes were cast against any person, the person was required to leave Athens for 10 years. Voters wrote the name of the person they wanted banished on pieces of clay called *ostraca.* Today, the English verb "ostracize" means "to banish or exclude an individual."

Patriot

The Latin word for father is *pater*. To refer to their capital city, the ancient Romans used *Roma*, but when they wished to refer to Rome as their homeland, their native country, they needed another term. Because they looked to the early founders of Rome as the fathers of Rome and Italy, it was only natural to use *pater* as a base. The result was *patria*, meaning "fatherland" or "homeland." English then borrowed *patria* and formed "patriot" to refer to a person who loyally defends and supports his or her country.

During the Civil War, colorful lithographic designs on envelopes bombarded the public with images of American flags, notable people, and historic events. The intent was to rally support and inspire patriotism.

Patron/Patronage

The words "patron" and "patronage" both trace their origins to the Latin noun *pater*, meaning "father." A patron shares many characteristics with a father: Both act as benefactors, protectors, supporters, and defenders. Patronage is the support or influence of such a person.

Plutocracy

A plutocracy is a government ruled by the wealthy. The term traces its roots to the Greek nouns *plutos*, meaning "wealth," and *kratos*, meaning "rule" or "strength." *Plutos*, in turn, traces its origins to Pluto, the god in ancient Greek and Roman mythology who ruled the underworld. Pluto became associated with wealth because of the rich mineral wealth found below the earth.

Political

The ancient Greeks used their word *polis*, meaning "city," to form the noun *polites*, meaning "citizen." Centuries later, English borrowed the word *polites* to form the adjective "political." It describes people and events involved in government.

Poll

Centuries ago, *pol* (also spelled *polle*) meant "head" or, more exactly, "the top of the head." Officials would travel from village to village to take a count of heads (*pols*) of people who favored or opposed a law or a candidate for office. Gradually, "poll" came to refer to votes both in an election and in an opinion survey.

A poll tax is usually a set fee placed on a person before he or she is allowed to vote. The imposition of this kind of tax has sparked several rebellions, including the Peasants' Revolt in England in 1381. Peasants had little money, and the poll tax kept them from voting. In recent times, it contributed to voter dissatisfaction with Margaret Thatcher, England's prime minister in the 1980s.

Protocol

Centuries ago, the Greeks followed the practice of attaching a *protokollon* to the front of a manuscript. On this they described the contents of the manuscript. *Protokollon* meant "first" (*protos*) "glue" (*kolla*). English adapted *protokollon* to "protocol" and used it to refer to the original record of a document. "Protocol" later came to mean a diplomatic agreement. Its third meaning, however, is the most familiar, which is the correct behavior used in meetings between heads of state or public officials.

One of the first ladies of protocol, Esther Pauline Friedman Lederer, published her first column in the Chicago *Sun-Times* in 1955. The column ran until her death in 2002. She was better known as Ann Landers.

Rostrum

To commemorate the great naval victory at Antium in 338 B.C., the Romans took the beaks or rams of the captured vessels to Rome and attached them to the speakers' platform in the Forum. As the Latin term for "beak of ship" was *rostrum,* from the verb *rodere ("to gnaw"),* the platform gradually came to be known as the *rostra* (plural of *rostrum*). English adopted the term to refer to the platform used for public speeches.

Senate/Senator

For the ancient Romans, the root word for "senate" and "senator" is *senex*, meaning "an old man." For the Romans, the senate was originally a council of elders or wise old men whose duty it was to administer the government.

While the duties of today's senators are comparable to those in ancient Rome, age and sex factors are no longer accurate. Many of today's senators are young—by ancient Rome's standards—and a significant number are women

Subpoena

This word is a combination of two Latin words: the preposition *sub* ("under") and the noun *poena* ("punishment" or "penalty"). Long after the fall of Rome in the year 476, Latin continued as the language used in universities and in the courtroom. Because many of those who were summoned to court failed to appear, a legal paper known as *sub poena ad testificandum* ("under penalty for the purpose of testifying") was issued to those whom the judge wished to have appear. Failure to obey the *sub poena* resulted in a penalty. Today, lawyers and courts continue to use the phrase with only one change: "Subpoena" is now written as one word.

Sultan

From the Arabic term *sultan,* meaning "prince" or "ruler," a sultan is a Muslim ruler with political power over his subjects. The rulers of the 16th-century Ottoman Empire of the Turks were known by the title of Sultan (with a capital S).

The last Ottoman Sultan was Muhammad VI. He was forced to abdicate in 1922 after soldier, statesman, and reformer Kemal Ataturk proclaimed Turkey a republic and became its first president.

Tsar

On March 15, 44 B.C, assassins killed the Roman leader Julius Caesar. Soon after, the Roman Senate decreed that his spirit be honored as divine. Caesar's successors wanted to link his name with their own, especially those who traced their descendants to Caesar or his family. In the following centuries, emperors who were not related to Caesar took the throne. They too incorporated the name "Caesar" into their titles. In 1547, Ivan IV became the first Russian ruler to assume the title of Caesar, pronounced *tsesar* in Russian. Derivatives of *tsesar* soon followed: *tsarina* for the tsar's wife, *tsarevitch* for his son, and *tsarevna* for his daughter. In English, the word became "tsar." It is also spelled "czar."

The last Russian tsar was Nicholas II. He was forced to abdicate in 1917. Shortly thereafter, he and his family were executed.

Military Madness

Don't "torpedo" this chapter before you even get started. "March" full speed ahead and prepare to "battle" with these "military" words without becoming "belligerent."

Admiral

This noun traces its origins to the Middle East. During the Middle Ages, Arabs used the term *amir* to refer to a chief and the phrase *amir-al-bahr* to refer to a chief on the sea. In the 11th, 12th, and 13th centuries, many of the Crusaders returning from the Middle East brought new words and phrases to their countries. Among these was *amir-al-bahr,* which became "admiral" in English.

Battle

"Battle" is a derivative of the late Latin terms *battuere,* meaning "to beat," and *battualia,* which describes the fighting and fencing exercises of soldiers and gladiators.

The battle between the Greeks and the Persians gave birth to the Delian League, an alliance of Greek city-states founded in 448–447 B.C. League members pledged to rally their forces and resources against their common enemy—the Persians.

Belligerent

A very descriptive adjective, "belligerent" refers to a person who always seems to be ready for a war or a fight. This definition fits the term, since it is a combination of two Latin words: the noun *bellum,* meaning "war," and the participle *gerens,* meaning "carrying on" or "waging."

Besiege

This verb traces its roots to the Old French *sieger*, meaning "to sit." To form *sieger*, the French adapted the Latin verb *sedere*, which also means "to sit." English then added the prefix *be*, meaning "by" or "around." Thus, besieging soldiers do exactly what the roots of the word say: They sit by or around an enemy city or town until the defenders surrender.

One of the most significant military confrontations in documented history was the siege of the Spanish town of Saguntum by the Carthaginian general Hannibal. In 219 B.C., after being besieged for almost a year, the inhabitants surrendered. Their defeat, as allies of Rome, led to the Second Punic War.

Blitzkrieg

The German term *blitzkrieg* is used to refer to an attack or war that is quick and intense. Appropriately, it is a combination of two German nouns: *blitz*, meaning "lightning," and *krieg*, meaning "war."

Buccaneer

"Buccaneer" brings to mind fierce pirates raiding the American coastal areas in the 1600s. Its origin, however, is quite unrelated to this dashing image. Early French hunters and explorers in South America and the Caribbean, especially the island of Hispaniola, often saw native people smoking meat over a fire on a wooden frame rack. They began to use the same method to cook their meat and also borrowed the native term for the process, adapting it to *boucan*. When the French began to sell the smoked meat, they quickly became known as *boucaniers*. However, because their activities also included raiding ventures, the meaning gradually changed to its present definition.

Bugle

For centuries, farmers, herdsman, and soldiers cleaned the horns of dead wild oxen and buffalo and used them as a type of whistle to round up animals or rally troops by blowing air through the narrow opening at the base. "Bugle" traces its roots to the Latin nouns *bos,* meaning "ox," and *buculus,* meaning "little ox." The early French changed *buculus* to *bugle* and used it to mean "buffalo." English adopted the French term and called the instrument made from the animal's horn a bugle-horn. In time, the phrase was shortened to "bugle."

Captain

The captain of a ship is the commanding officer, the one who leads the crew. This title traces its roots to the Latin noun *caput,* meaning "head." Another English derivative is **capital,** a city or town that is the official seat of government of a state, nation, or empire.

Castle

A castle is a large building or group of buildings fortified for defense against an enemy. The Norman conquerors built stone castles all over England for protection. Before the year 1000, English use of the medieval Latin *castel* referred to a village. After the Norman Conquest of England in 1066, the sense of *castel* as a fortress came into English from Old Northern French. Many English castles were indeed stone villages.

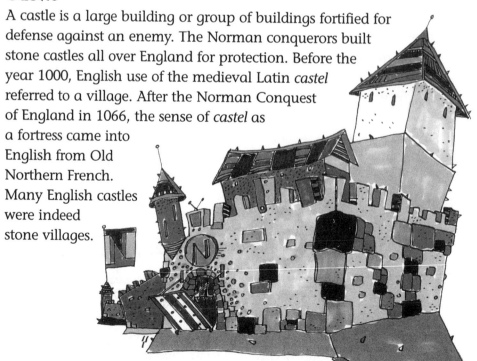

Colonel

"Colonel" traces its origin through the Italian noun *colonello*, meaning "the chief commander of a regiment," to the Latin noun *columna*, meaning "column" or "pillar." Hence, a colonel is considered a pillar of strength by his soldiers.

Defeat

This word traces it roots through the Old French past participle *desfait*, meaning "undone," to two Latin terms: *dis* ("apart" or "in different directions") and *facere* ("to do" or "to make"). Thus, anyone who is made to go in different directions is a person who has been destroyed, undone, or conquered.

In ancient Greece, when one side in a battle wished to surrender and admit defeat, a designated person would wave an olive branch so that the enemy could see it. In time, the olive branch became regarded as a universal symbol for peace.

Fleet

In Old English (spoken from about the years 100 to 400), *fleotan* meant "to float." As the centuries passed, *fleotan* gradually changed to *fleote*, and then finally to "fleet." The meaning broadened, and "fleet" came to mean "to drift" and "to flow." Soon "fleet" became a noun as well as a verb and was used to refer to something that floats. The next step was easy—a fleet was a group of boats under one command.

By the time of the First Punic War (264–241 B.C.), Rome's fleet of warships numbered more than 200 quinqueremes (ships with five banks of oars).

Greek fire

The rulers of Constantinople never invested great sums of money in a navy to protect the area or the ports and waters of the Byzantine Empire. If necessary, merchant ships could be refitted to serve as warships. Aware that this strategy was not always successful, the Byzantine military relied heavily on a seventh-century invention called "Greek fire." The exact composition of Greek fire was a well-guarded secret, but military experts believe it contained a combination of various chemicals, possibly naphtha, saltpeter, and/or sulfur. The Byzantines encased this compound in a clay container before catapulting it in a gun-like tube at the enemy. It exploded on impact, burning everything it touched, even water. Greek fire was generally confined to naval warfare, since commanders knew the disastrous consequences of an accident in camp or on a march.

Byzantine princess Anna Comnena wrote a vivid description of Greek fire that was used by her father's fleet. Because the emperor Alexius I Comnenus (1081–1118) feared the naval power of the people of Pisa, Italy, he ordered a gilded bronze or iron head of a lion or some such animal to be affixed to the prow of each Byzantine warship. The mouth of the animal was to be constructed as a hole through which Greek fire could be squirted. This would make the enemy think the animals were vomiting or breathing fire.

Grenade

The Romans enjoyed eating the fruit we call pomegranate. Except for the fact that it was full of seeds, they thought it resembled an apple and named it *pomum granatum,* "an apple having seeds." The French borrowed the term, changing the spelling to *pome grenate.* When a small bomb filled with explosives was invented, the French called it a *grenade,* because it exploded into so many "seeds." The word came into English unchanged.

Guerrilla

Through the centuries, countless individuals have waged skirmishes, battles, and even wars against government military forces. Their organization is not as tight as that of official military troops, and their tactics are quick, offensive movements rather than prolonged, strategic battles. The type of warfare is often unpredictable and conducted in areas of rough terrain. The Spanish used their word for war, *guerra,* to refer to the type of individual who fights in this manner. In Spanish, the suffix *illa* means "little." Hence, "guerrilla" literally means "little war."

In 1959, Fidel Castro used guerrilla forces to overthrow Cuba's leader, Fulgencio Baptista. Castro remains in power today.

Gun

In 1330, an inventory was taken of all the weapons housed at England's Windsor Castle, just outside London. Among those listed was a large ballista called Lady Gunhilda. While it is known that the ballista was used to hurl heavy stones and similar missiles, exactly how this weapon received its name is unknown. Soldiers often nicknamed the arms they used, and "Gunhilda" is actually a combination of two Old Norse words: *gunnr,* meaning "war," and *hildr,* meaning "battle." As the years passed, "gunhilda" was accepted as the name of a firearm. In time, it was shortened to *gunne* and then to our modern-day "gun."

Early handguns were little more than portable cannon. Muzzle-loaded and lit with a match, they were inaccurate and slow.

infantry

The Romans combined their preposition *in,* meaning "not," with their present participle *fans,* meaning "speaking," to form the noun *infans* ("an infant"). The Italians used their forebears' term as the root of two related ideas. *Infante* adopted the Latin meaning and described a "baby" or "small child," while *infanteria* referred to those individuals in the military who were considered inexperienced and unqualified for cavalry duty. "Infantry," the English derivative of *infans,* adopted still another meaning, as it refers to soldiers equipped for service on foot.

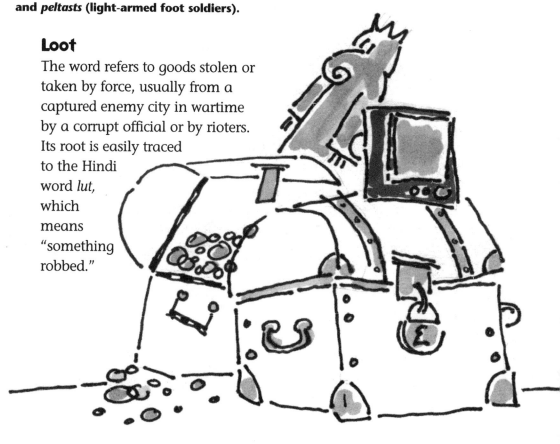

The Greek term *hoplites* refers to the heavily armored infantry the ancient Greek city-states employed as regular troops. Other types of Greek infantry included the *phalangites* (soldiers in the phalanx formation), *hypaspists* (shield-bearers), and *peltasts* (light-armed foot soldiers).

Loot

The word refers to goods stolen or taken by force, usually from a captured enemy city in wartime by a corrupt official or by rioters. Its root is easily traced to the Hindi word *lut,* which means "something robbed."

Mail

Mail is the flexible body armor that knights in the Middle Ages and the early Renaissance wore into battle. Because the small interlocking iron rings resembled a fishnet, those who fashioned the armor called it *maille*, the Old French word for "link" or "net." Tracing *maille*'s roots further, it derives from the Latin noun *macula*, which the ancient Romans used to describe the mesh of a net. Today, "mail" most often describes letters or messages that we receive from others. This version of the word comes the Old French *male*, meaning "pouch."

On May 1, 1840, the first adhesive postage stamp went on sale in Great Britain. The stamp was named "Penny Black" and had the head of England's Queen Victoria on it.

Maneuver

Since "maneuver" incorporates the French noun *oeuvre*, meaning "work," into its form, it is commonly accepted as an English term borrowed from the French vocabulary. But few people know of its classical roots. Late Latin used the classical Latin terms *manu* ("by hand") and *operari* ("to work") to form the noun *manuopera*, a term that designated "handwork" or "manual labor." The French replaced the form *opera* with their term for work, *oeuvre*, and the English Anglicized the French word. In earlier times, "maneuver" was used to refer to a hand laborer. Today, it is most commonly associated with military and naval tactics and strategies.

March

In the early Roman calendar, March was the first month of the year and the time when military campaigns began. (Around 45 B.C., Julius Caesar revised the calendar, making January the first month and March the third month.) Since March was when fair weather returned to the Roman world, it had always been considered the perfect time to go to battle. The Romans had named the month in honor of their god of war, Mars.

Military

This English word for members of the armed forces comes directly from the Latin noun for soldier, *miles* (the plural is *milites*). **Militant, militarism,** and **militia** also trace their roots to *miles*. "Militant" means "fighting or warring" or "having a combative character." "Militarism" describes holding up the ideals of a professional military class. A "militia" is an emergency military force consisting of ordinary citizens rather than professional soldiers.

Pirate

Pirates were a great menace on the ancient seas. To label individuals who attacked others, or attempted to, the Greeks used their verb *peiran,* meaning "to attempt to attack," and formed *peirates.* The Romans adapted the form to *piratae,* the precursor of the English term.

Strategy

Derived from a combination of the Greek noun *stratos,* meaning "army," and the Greek verb *agein,* meaning "to lead," "strategy" refers to the art of planning a scheme whereby one army is able to deceive and trick another army.

Alexander the Great (356–323 B.C.) is still admired today as an exceptional leader and an expert in military strategy. Although he died before the age of 33, he conquered most of the regions of the Middle East, Greece, Turkey, and Egypt and changed the direction of history.

Subjugate

When farmers want two draft animals, especially oxen, to work together at a chore, they harness them together with a bar or wooden frame that has a loop at either end for each animal's head. In English, this device is known as a yoke. The ancient Romans called it *iugum,* a derivative of their verb *iungere,* meaning "to join." When the Romans began conquering other nations, they sought some punishment for the defeated people that would symbolize Roman domination. They adopted a customary practice from ancient times. After assembling the defeated troops, the Romans stuck two spears upright in the ground and laid a third across them. The conquered army was then forced to pass beneath this "yoke," symbolically acknowledging their position as slaves to their conquerors. The Romans termed this humiliating experience *sub iugum* ("under the yoke"), from which was derived "subjugate," meaning "to conquer" or "to subdue."

Submarine

The submarine does exactly what its name says it does. *Sub* is the Latin preposition for "under" and *mare* is the Latin noun for "sea."

English often uses the Latin preposition *sub* ("under") as a prefix. For example, a subway is an underground train system, and subterranean describes something lying under the earth's surface.

Torpedo

The Romans coined the noun *torpedo* from their verb *torpere,* (meaning "to be stiff" or "to be numb") to name the species of fish that produces electrical discharges. They did so because anyone stung by this type of fish felt stiff or numb. In the late 18th century, the term was used to refer to the manmade shell that shoots through the water and explodes upon contact with a hard object.

Tantalizing Tidbits

Don't "panic" at the "scope" of this chapter. Read it through with "enthusiasm" and you will ultimately "astonish" and "tantalize" your friends with your descriptive vocabulary.

Abominable

The ancient Romans did not look forward to an omen or a sign of a future event, since it often foretold evil. Hence, the adjective "abominable" (meaning "loathsome" or "unpleasant") appropriately traces its roots to the Latin preposition *ab* ("away from") and the Latin noun *omen* ("sign of future events or happenings").

Achieve

This commonly used English verb traces its roots to the Latin phrase *ad caput venire,* "to come to a head or peak" or "to end." In ancient times the Romans occasionally used this expression when referring to death and dying since, at that point, a person's life does come to an end. The early French translated this phrase into their language as *venir à chief.* In time these three words blended together to form the French verb *achever,* "to finish," which later passed into English as "achieve." Until as late as the 16th century and the time of the English playwright William Shakespeare (1564–1616), "achieve" still connoted the idea of "to die" or "to kill." Gradually it assumed its present meaning, which is "to bring to successful conclusion," "to perform," or "to attain."

The first person under the age of 18 to win a gold medal in the Olympics was the coxswain of the Netherlands at the 1900 games in Paris, France. The coxswain sits in the back of a shell (a long, narrow, thin-hulled racing boat) and calls out the rowing rhythm for the crew.

Agony

The Greeks used *agonia* to denote an athletic contest and *agon* to refer to the place where the contest was held. Since the majority of participants in athletic contests lose their bid for first prize, *agonia* gradually came to mean "heartbreak" and "intense suffering," both mental and physical. The word became "agony" in English.

Ambitious

The Latin word *ambitio* meant "going around" and is from *ambi* ("around" or "on both sides") and *itus* ("having gone"). In every-day speech, the Romans used *ambitio* to refer to politicians who made the rounds soliciting votes. Through the centuries, English adapted the meaning to refer to any individual who exhibits a strong desire to succeed.

Anecdote

By definition, "anecdote" is a biographical or historical fact that is little-known and amusing. Its roots are the Greek prefixes *an* ("not") and *ek* ("out") and the Greek verb *didonai* ("to give"). Thus, an anecdote literally means something not given out, or something unpublished.

Invention Anecdote: The first slide fastener was invented in 1893 and exhibited at the World's Fair that same year by Whitcomb Judson. In 1913, the device gained teeth and became what we now know as a zipper.

Aroma

An aroma is a pleasant odor or fragrance. English borrowed the term from the Old French *aromat*, meaning "sweet spice."

Asterisk

The star-shaped symbol the asterisk is used to indicate additional information, a footnote, or an explanation somewhere relatively close or on the same page. "Asterisk" traces its roots to the Greek nouns *aster* ("star") and *asteriskos* ("little star").

Astonished

An astonished person is one who is surprised or amazed. Yet this word originally had a stronger meaning. "Astonished" actually means "thunderstruck." It derives from two Latin words: the preposition *ex*, meaning "out," and the verb *tonare*, meaning "to thunder."

Auspicious

The Etruscans and Romans believed strongly in divination, the art of foretelling events. It was common practice to watch the actions of birds and from them predict whether a proposed undertaking should be approved or denied. To name the religious people in charge of watching and interpreting the flights of birds, the ancients combined their noun *avis* ("bird") and verb *spectare* ("to watch") to form *auspices*. What the *auspices* did was called *auspicium*. English later borrowed *auspices* and made it into the adjective "auspicious," meaning "favorable" in the sense of "a good sign."

The Romans believed that the gods communicated their will and desires through oracles, strange sights, events, and coincidences—such as the flight patterns of birds.

Beauty

The Romans used the adjective *bellus* to describe something that was beautiful. But *bellus* meant more than beautiful to the Romans, for they had adapted their adjective *benulus* to form *bellus*. *Benulus* was derived from *bonus,* the Latin adjective for "good." Hence, *bellus* implied that if something were beautiful, it should also be good. The early French adapted *bellus* to form the adjectives *beau* (masculine) and *belle* (feminine), meaning "fine" and "beautiful." The English changed the French word and formed "beauty."

Aphrodite was the Greek goddess of love and beauty. The Romans knew her as Venus.

Candice

The Meroitic (from Meroë in Nubia) word for queen is *kandake*, and has come down to us as the girl's name "Candice."

Companion

This English noun traces its roots to two Latin words: the preposition *cum*, meaning "with," and the noun *panis*, meaning "bread." Thus, a companion originally was someone with whom you shared your bread or food, especially while traveling or in military barracks. Related to companion is the English word **company**, which still, by definition, refers to individuals who share food and/or conversation socially.

Consider

Seeking the advice of gods and goddesses before embarking on any important venture was a common practice in the Greek and Roman worlds. One way to do so was by observing the movement and alignment of constellations and planets. To describe these consultations, the Romans used the verb *considerare*, a combination of the preposition *cum* ("with") and the noun *sidus* ("constellation"). Since interpreting the stars required much thought and careful observation, *considerare* soon acquired a second meaning—"to look at closely." It is this second meaning that came into English as the definition of the verb "consider."

The Greek astronomer Hipparchus of Rhodes compiled the first known catalog or list of the stars around 127 B.C.

Delirious

"Delirious" is defined as "wildly excited" or "rambling and raving incoherently." It literally means "away from the furrow," and traces its roots to the Latin adjective *delirius* ("silly" or "crazy"). To refer to people who seemed out of their senses, the ancient Romans combined the preposition *de* ("away with") with *lira*, their noun for "furrow" or "row." Anyone who acted in a bizarre manner was like a farmer who plowed outside the furrows in a field.

Desire

"Desire" traces its roots to the Latin noun *sidera,* meaning "stars." *De* is a Latin preposition meaning "from" and is often used as a prefix. In English, "desire" means "to want," a definition that implies a person is lacking something—that is, he or she is away from his or her lucky stars.

Elizabeth Blackwell finally found her "lucky stars" in 1848. After numerous rejections, Blackwell was accepted by Geneva Medical College in New York to fulfill her desire to be the first woman in the United States to graduate from a medical school.

Diehard

The British 57th Regiment of Foot, known as the Die Hards, had a reputation for fierce loyalty, due mostly to its commanding officer. At the Battle of Albuera in 1811, the officer, though wounded, cried out to his men, "Die hard, 57th, die hard." During the Sepoy Rebellion in India in 1857–58, the soldiers of the 57th again proved their loyalty in a critical battle. The term soon moved beyond the battlefield to describe a very stubborn person.

Disaster

A compound of the Latin prefix *de,* meaning "apart" or "away from," and *aster,* meaning "star," "disaster" literally refers to an event that occurs when the stars are out of their proper sequence.

One of the great disasters of the Roman Empire was the Great Fire in the year 64. It ravaged almost three-quarters of Rome, the empire's capital, and went on for nine days and nights.

Enthusiasm

This noun actually has religious roots. A combination of the Greek prefix *en* ("in") and the Greek noun *theos* ("god"), "enthusiasm" originally referred to someone who was inspired or possessed from within by a god. This person was usually a fanatic, someone whose adherence to religious belief went beyond the reasonable. In time, this meaning was lost and enthusiasm came to mean "a feeling of intense interest or great eagerness."

Excerpt

An excerpt is a passage or quotation selected from a book, article, or other source. It is a derivative of the Latin preposition *ex*, meaning "out of," and the Latin participle *carptum*, meaning "picked" or "chosen."

Expert

Used both as an adjective and a noun to denote someone highly skilled in a particular field, "expert" traces its roots to the Latin verb *experiri*, meaning "to put to the test" or "to know by experience." *Experiri*, in turn, traces its roots to the Latin adjective *peritum* ("skillful") and the Latin noun *periculum* ("danger"). Thus, experts are people who prove their skill in a field after being put to the test under circumstances that may involve danger.

Glamour

That "grammar" and "glamour" can be related seems hardly possible, but the two words do have the same root: the Greek noun *gramma,* meaning "letter." It is only in recent history that reading has become widespread. Even as recently as the mid-1500s, few people in Europe had learned to read or write. As a result, words seemed mysterious and magical to most people. Those who did read knew Latin, which had become one of the world's international languages. However, as the decades passed, fewer and fewer people knew or studied the rules of Latin grammar. Consequently, the ability to converse in Latin often was associated with black magic. During the Middle Ages, English used the term *gramarye* to mean "magic." In time, the letter "r" changed to "l." This new derivative, *glamarye,* first meant "magic," "spell," or "charm." Gradually, it lost its close association with black magic and came to mean the "captivating charm a particular person possesses."

Even in ancient Greece glamour was a must. Women used psimythion (white lead) to whiten their faces, rouge from plants to highlight their cheeks, and kohl to darken their eyelids.

Hazard

"Risk," "chance," and "danger"—these three words all define the English term "hazard." Its roots do the same, since hazard traces its origin to the Arabic article *al* ("the") and the Arabic noun *zahr* ("die"). Throwing dice (the plural of "die") involves chance and the unknown. Other languages also adapted *al-zahr.* For example, in Spanish it became *azar,* "an unexpected accident."

Hearse

Iron candelabra-type forms that were used in past centuries to hold candles in churches resembled the *hirpex,* which is the Latin word for "a large rake." The French adapted the word to *herce* and it was applied to the frame supporting funeral candles and then to the vehicle that carries the coffin to the gravesite.

Heckler

A heckler is someone who harasses and annoys another person with questions or scornful remarks. The link to the original meaning of the word is obvious once you know that in the 13th century a heckle (also spelled "hackle") was an instrument used to untangle, separate, and straighten fibers of flax (used for making linen) and hemp (used for making rope). To heckle the fibers was actually to tease them so that they might act as the worker wished.

Hectic

The ancient Greeks used their verb *exein* ("to have" and "to hold") as the root of the noun *hexis,* meaning "something that was held or done again and again" or "a habit" and the adjective *hektikos,* meaning "habitual." In time, *hektikos* came to refer to tuberculosis (also known as TB), a dreaded sickness that caused hot, dry skin, flushed cheeks, and a fever that kept recurring. English adapted *hektikos* to "hectic" and gradually modified the meaning to refer to feverish activity or action that is characterized by confusion and excitement.

Histrionics

In Latin, an actor was referred to as a *histrio* (the plural is *histriones*). Some etymologists believe that the Romans borrowed this term from the Etruscans, their neighbors to the north, who became subject to Roman authority in the fourth century B.C. While the Etruscan language has not yet been deciphered, the meanings of some words are known. It is believed that *histrio* is a form of the Etruscan *hister,* meaning "an individual who earns his living by amusing others with tricks, a clown." In the 16th and 17th centuries, *histrio* and *histrion* were commonly used in English to designate an actor. Today, "histrionics" has contemptuous connotations and is generally used to express overreacting and affected behavior.

The Etruscans were the inhabitants of ancient Etruria, in central Italy, and established a thriving farming and commercial civilization that peaked in the 6th century B.C. They are also known for their realistic wall paintings.

Hypocrite

Oftentimes, as a word passes from region to region and generation to generation, its meaning changes considerably. Such was the case with "hypocrite." Centuries ago, when the Greeks sought a word to represent the dramatic character on stage who decided what action to take or disputed what his fellow performers said, they joined the prefix *hypo* ("under") with the verb *krinein* ("to decide" or "to dispute"). The result was *hypocrites*. Aware that an actor generally assumes the identity of someone other than himself, English borrowed the Greek term *hypocrites* and used it to represent any individual who pretends to be either better or different than his or her true personality.

The first theater in Athens was built between 550 and 534 B.C. The early theaters were originally designed to host festivals in honor of Dionysus, the god of fruitfulness and pleasure.

Hysteria

The ancient Greeks considered emotions and personality traits all related to what went on inside the body. Anything that differed from normal behavior was attributed to a particular organ, an organic change, or an imbalance of the fluids that make up the body. Women were considered more emotional than men. The ancients attributed a woman's fickleness to the fact that she had a womb. The Greek term for womb was *hystera,* and the term for the emotional condition was *hysterikos.* Today, our derivative "hysteria" is not associated with men or women. It simply describes any outbreak of wild emotion.

idea

This English noun is actually a form of the Greek verb *idein,* meaning "to see." The ancients first had used *idein* to signify a "look," "form," or "outward appearance." As a result of the beliefs of the Greek philosopher Plato (427–347 B.C.), however, "idea" began to refer more to a person's conception of what was to come—that is, a person looked something over to see what it meant. Since the picture conceived in one's mind is usually better or of a more perfect nature than the actual object or fact, "idea" came to signify a thought or mental image. An English derivative of this Greek term is the word **ideal**, meaning "the perfect model."

Plato founded the Academy in Athens. Its pupils became some of Greece's most influential thinkers and statesmen. The Academy remained open for more than 900 years.

idiot

The ancient Greeks referred to a private person, that is, a person who held no public office, as an *idotes.* Gradually, the term came to mean "a foolish or stupid person." Scientifically, "idiot" refers to someone whose mental ability is equivalent to or less than that of a two-year-old.

187

innocent

This adjective traces its roots to *nocens,* the present participle of the Latin verb *nocere,* meaning "to harm." *In* is the prefix used by the Romans to indicate the negative of the term that followed. Hence, *in* plus *nocere* means "not to harm."

intrigue

When the Roman comic writer Plautus used the Latin verb *extricare* in a play, it meant to unravel the story or the plot. To form this term, the Romans had combined their preposition *ex* ("out") with their noun *tricae* ("trifling nonsense" or "troubles"). *Tricae* was, in turn, a derivative of the Greek *trichos* meaning "hair." The fact that anything that becomes entangled in hair is difficult to extricate must have contributed to *trichos* and *tricae* becoming the root for *intricare,* from which the French formed their verb *intriguer.* The French, however, altered the meaning by introducing the idea of secrecy, a concept which our English form of "intrigue" still retains.

The "king of intrigue" was Sir Arthur Conan Doyle of England, the author of the Sherlock Holmes detective series.

inundate

The English language combined the Latin noun *unda* (meaning "wave") with several Latin prepositions to form a variety of words. *Unda* plus *in* ("on") formed "inundate," meaning "to deluge" or "to flood." *Unda* plus *re* ("again") formed **redundant,** meaning "to flow or speak more than is necessary." *Unda* plus *ab* ("away") formed **abundant,** meaning "flowing away, plentiful."

Jeopardy

The Latin noun *iocus* meant "a joke," "a jest," or "a game." In time, the Romans coined the phrase *jocus partitus* to designate a drawn game, or a game that is even or tied. The French adopted the phrase, changed the spelling to *jeu parti,* and used it to represent evenly matched opponents as well. Since the outcome of a game that is tied or whose players are equally skilled is uncertain, *jeu parti,* gradually came to mean "uncertainty." English changed the French phrase to "jeopardy" and used it first in chess and other similar games. Time, however, strengthened the connotation of uncertainty to such an extent that "in jeopardy" has come to mean someone in extremely serious danger.

Many of us know *Jeopardy* as a time-tested quiz show. However, the very first quiz show aired on CBS TV on February 2, 1950. It was titled *What's My Line?*

Jovial

In early Roman mythology, Jovis was the king of the gods. His name later changed to Jupiter, a compound of Jovis and *pater,* the Latin noun for "father." In honor of the all-powerful god, ancient astronomers named the largest planet in the solar system Jupiter. After astrologists noted that individuals born under Jupiter's sign were happy and joyful, etymologists thought it fitting to use "jovial" to mean "genial" or "of good humor."

Laconic

The people of Sparta were widely known throughout the ancient Mediterranean world for their frugal ways. They never wasted anything, not even words. Ancient writers often referred to the Spartans as "Laconians," because Sparta was the chief city of the district of Laconia. In one account, a writer told of an Athenian envoy sent to Sparta with the message, "If we come to your city, we will destroy it." The Spartan reply was, "If." When speakers of English wanted an adjective that would convey the idea of speaking bluntly and with few words, they borrowed the name Laconia and formed the English term "laconic."

Nausea

Seasickness has plagued travelers for thousands of years. The ancient Greeks used the noun *naus*, meaning "ship," to form *nausia*, the Greek noun denoting the woozy feeling seasick people experience. *Naus* and *navis*, the Latin word for "ship," have become the root of several English seafaring terms, including **nautical** ("of or relating to ships, shipping, or sailors"), **navigate** ("to plan or control the course of a craft"), and **navy** ("a group of ships").

Obituary

Newspapers carry death notices accompanied by brief biographies of people. In English, this type of column is called an obituary. The term is a direct derivative of the Latin participle *obitum*, which means "having gone over."

Optimist/Pessimist

"Optimist" traces its roots to *optimus*, meaning "best." "Pessimist" traces its roots to *pessimus*, meaning "worst." An optimist always anticipates the best in any situation while a pessimist prepares for the worst.

Panic

The ancient Greeks believed that a woodland deity named Pan enjoyed making horrible noises, especially at night, to frighten people. They called the fear he caused *deima panikon*, meaning "Panic fear." In English, "panic" is used to describe a sudden, overwhelming fear that has no basis.

Persecute

This Anglicized form of the French verb *persécuter* is a combination of the Latin preposition *per* ("through") and the participle *secutus* ("followed"). To persecute someone is to harass that person constantly, especially for religious, political, or racial reasons.

Phineas

In the Bible, the grandson of Aaron and the son of Eli both have the name Phineas. Egyptologists believe that the root of "Phineas" is an Egyptian proper name frequently used during the New Kingdom (c. 1570–1070 B.C.), *Paneshsy,* meaning "the Nubian." The name became very popular in 17th century England.

Phobia

Derived from the Greek noun *phobos,* meaning "fear," "phobia" refers to an exaggerated and unexplainable fear of something. To name a specific fear, English often combines "phobia" with a variety of other prefixes, many of which are also Greek words. **Acrophobia** (*akros* is Greek for "height") means a fear of great height. **Agoraphobia** (*agora* is Greek for "assembly place" or "marketplace") is a fear of crossing or being in the middle of open spaces. **Claustrophobia** (*claustrum* is Latin for "an enclosure") is a fear of being in a closed room or narrow space. **Hydrophobia** (*hydor* is Greek for "water") is a fear of water. **Pyrophobia** (*pyr* is Greek for "fire") is a fear of fire.

Pyre

While every language has terms and phrases peculiar to its own vocabulary or to a particular region where a dialect is spoken, a form to express the concept of fire exists in every language. In Greek, the word is *pyr,* which has become the basis for several English words. A pyre is a combustible heap, often of wood, used for burning a dead body as a funeral rite. **Empyreal** pertains to the highest heaven, which was once thought to consist of fire and light. **Pyretology** is the branch of medicine that treats fevers. **Pyrex** is a trademark applied to a variety of glassware that is resistant to heat, chemicals, and electricity. **Pyromania** is the uncontrollable impulse to start fires (*mania* is Greek for "madness"). **Pyrosis** is a disorder of the stomach, or heartburn.

Quixotic

The Spanish novelist Miguel de Cervantes (1547–1616) named his chief work after its main character, Don Quixote. Quixote tried to be the perfect knight, but he was far too idealistic and impractical and, as a result, behaved foolishly. English borrowed his name, made it an adjective— "quixotic"— and used it to refer to any person who behaves like Don Quixote.

Résumé

The French use *résumé* to connote "a summary" or "a summing up of ideas." The English definition is basically the same. However, in English, a résumé generally refers to the written profile of the significant history and achievements in a person's life. This profile is kept updated and submitted whenever a person applies for a job or a promotion. The term traces its roots to the Latin prefix *re*, meaning "back" or "again," and the Latin verb *sumere*, meaning "to take."

Rigmarole

Today, "rigmarole" means "foolish talk or time-wasting procedures that do not make sense." While its exact origin is uncertain, its history is linked to the 1290s when King Edward I of England took control of Scotland and had the nobles and landowners sign a document pledging their allegiance to him. This document was known as a ragman roll (why is not known). As the lists of names were hurriedly obtained, not all the writing was legible. Nor was the document in good order. The phrase "ragman roll" soon came to mean "a jumble of words." In time, it was corrupted to "rigmarole."

Scapegoat

Today a scapegoat is a person who is made to take the blame for a crime or mistake committed by another person. In ancient times, for members of the Jewish faith, a scapegoat was an actual goat. According to the law of Moses, during the festival of Yom Kippur two goats were led to the altar of the tabernacle. Lots were cast to see which goat was to be sacrificed and which goat was to be the scapegoat. The high priest would then confess the sins of the people over the scapegoat's head before it was allowed to escape into the wilderness carrying all these sins on its head.

Scent

"Scent" is from the Old French verb *sentir,* meaning "to feel." It describes a fragrance or perfume.

Scope

The dictionary defines "scope" as "the range of understanding." The term is from the Greek verb *skopein,* meaning "to look attentively." In English, it is often combined with other Greek terms to form many words. A **horoscope** (*horo* is Greek for "hour" or "season") is an astrological forecast of a person's future based on a diagram of the planets and stars. A **kaleidoscope** (*kalos* is Greek for "beautiful" and *eidos* is Greek for "form") is an optical instrument that offers constantly changing patterns by rotating the bits of colored glass inside it. A **microscope** (*mikros* is Greek for "small") is an optical instrument used to magnify images of small objects. A **telescope** (*tele* is Greek for "far off") is an optical instrument used to help a person see something at a distance.

Susan

This feminine proper name has deep roots. English borrowed the Latin name *Susanna,* which was the Latinized form of the Greek *Sousanna.* The latter appears as the name of the wife of Joakin, ruler of Judah, in an early Greek translation of the Bible. The Greek spelling was an adaptation of the Hebrew *Shushanna,* the feminine form of *shushan.* The meaning of *shushan* can be traced to the Egyptian word for the lotus flower, *shoshen.* The Egyptians highly prized the beautiful, sweet-smelling blue lotus, and *shoshen* became the root of the flower's name in several Eastern languages. In Greek, it was *souson.*

Talent

For the ancient Greeks, the term *talanton* represented a specific weight and monetary unit whose estimated value varied, as does the value of our currency today. The Romans later adopted the Greek term and changed it to *talentum.* Its present significance came as a result of a story found in the New Testament. According to Matthew 25: 14–46, a man distributed his goods among his servants: "to one he gave five talents; to another two; and to another one; to every man according to his abilities." Hence, "talent" now means "superior intelligence and ability" and "a natural capacity or gift."

Some say that U.S. athlete Jim Thorpe (1888–1953) was the most talented all-around athlete in history. He won the pentathlon and the decathlon at the 1912 Olympic Games, and, in 1950, the Associated Press named him the greatest U.S. athlete in the first half of the 20th century.

Tantalize

The ancient Greeks believed that Zeus punished any god or super-human who abused his own powers or the powers of his fellow deities. Tantalus, the king of an area in Asia Minor (present-day Turkey), was one such person. Zeus confined Tantalus to a pool of cool, refreshing water surrounded by fruit trees. The beautiful setting deceived Tantalus. Whenever he went to drink the water, it receded. Whenever he reached for the luscious fruit hanging above his head, it, too, moved beyond his reach. Thus Tantalus gave his name to "tantalize," meaning "to tease" by not allowing someone to have what he or she wants even though it is readily available. *See also* **tantalum** *(page 41).*

The Romans identified many of the Greek gods with their gods. Sometimes, they kept the Greek name, as with Apollo. Other times, they used the Roman name. The Greek god Zeus was the Roman god Jupiter.

Vernacular

The Latin noun *verna,* which may be Etruscan in origin, was commonly used in ancient times to designate "a slave born in his master's house." The adjective *vernacula* gradually came into use to refer to anything pertaining to such a slave. In time, it came to mean "domestic" and was used with the Latin noun *vocabula,* meaning "name." Gradually, the meaning of the phrase *vernacula vocabula* changed to "native languages." Then, sometime later, *vocabula* was dropped and *vernacula* became "vernacular," a term used primarily to refer to native languages or dialects.

Victoria

The proper name "Victoria" is actually a Latin word that means "victory." To form *victoria,* the Romans adapted their noun *victor,* Latin for "one who conquers."

Fickle Finances

Did you know that the origins of the word for "salary" comes from Roman times and means a "salt allowance"? At one time, salt was a valuable commodity. Are you "worth your salt"? (See page 89 for an explanation of that saying.)

Assistant

Derived from the Latin prepositions *ad* ("to") and *stans* ("standing"), an assistant is one who stands by and helps someone else.

Bankrupt

In medieval Italy, moneylenders operated from *bancas,* meaning "benches" or "shelves." When a moneylender was forced to suspend business because of lack of funds, his *banca* was disbanded and he was labeled a *bancarotto.* The term *bancarotto* became "bankrupt" in English and gradually came to refer to those who legally declare themselves incapable of paying their debts.

In 1958, the first credit card, the Bank Americard, was introduced by the Bank of America.

Bill

"Bill" traces its origins to *bulla,* the name of the round, bubble-like locket worn by Roman children. The *bulla's* shape gradually made its name synonymous with the round bubble that was used to seal official documents in the Middle Ages. In time, the spelling changed to "bill," and its definition expanded to refer to a piece of paper money, an account of money owed, or a document.

Wearing a *bulla* fashioned of gold was a privilege granted only to Roman aristocrats. Children of poor families and freedmen wore a *bulla* made of leather.

Budget

Bulga was the term used by the Romans to represent a leather bag. The early French adopted the term, changing the spelling to *bouge.* The French later added the ending *tte* to form *bougette,* a term for a little bag or wallet. During the Middle Ages, it was customary for French merchants to carry their money in *bougettes.* When English adopted the term, the spelling was changed to "budget," and the definition greatly expanded. While "budget" formerly connoted a bag or a sack and its contents, today it describes a financial statement or estimated income and expenses.

Romans were generally careful bookkeepers and budgeters. A merchant kept a record of his accounts in a ledger called "the book of money received and the book of money paid." He used two columns for the record—just as we do today.

Cartel

"Cartel" traces its roots directly to the Latin noun *charta,* meaning "paper." Originally, it referred to a written challenge, as when one person challenged another to a duel. Then it came to mean a written agreement regarding an exchange of prisoners between nations that were at war. Today, "cartel" still refers to a written agreement, specifically one that trading partners have established to control prices or limit the output of a product (such as oil).

Dollar

Around 1516, a rich silver mine was discovered on an estate in a small town in Bohemia called Sankt Joachimsthal. The German name of the town translates into English as Saint Joachim's Valley. By 1518, one-ounce silver coins were being minted and put into circulation. Because the face or obverse side of the coin was imprinted with an image of St. Joachim, the coin came to be known as a *Joachimsthaler.* In time, the term was shortened to *thaler,* which was pronounced "daller" in northern Germany. By the late 1700s, the *thaler* had become a standard unit of currency used internationally. When the leaders of the new United States sought a name for their currency, they wanted to break completely with England and English influence. They chose a decimal system and adapted *thaler* to "dollar."

"Dollar diplomacy" is a term used to describe the United States' policy of economic and military interference in Latin America in the early 1900s.

Kiosk

From the Turkish word *kosk,* meaning "pavilion," "kiosk" describes a summerhouse or small outdoor structure, usually with open sides that was common in Turkey and Iran. The French adapted the Turkish term to *kiosque* and used it to refer to a small open structure such as a newsstand or bandstand. The English adopted the French meaning and Anglicized it to "kiosk."

Money

The Roman goddess Juno, queen of the gods and goddesses, was considered the patroness of marriage and childbirth and the protector of young maidens. The Romans also worshiped her as the goddess of warning because tradition held that Juno had, on many occasions, been responsible for warning the people of Rome of imminent danger. Consequently, they dedicated a temple to her on Rome's Capitoline Hill. Juno's epithet as the goddess of warning was *Moneta,* from the verb *monere,* meaning "to warn." Housed in a building adjoining Juno's temple was Rome's mint, the place where the money was coined. Gradually, the term *moneta* assumed a new definition and came to mean the mint itself. *Moneta* entered the French language as *moneie,* from which comes "money." A **mint,** used to designate a place where the money is coined, also traces its origin to Juno's epithet *Moneta.*

The Greek writer Xenophanes (active around 520 B.C.) noted that the Lydians in Asia Minor (present-day Turkey) were the first to make and use coins. The value of coined money was determined by weight.

Negotiate

This term traces its origin to the Latin words *nec,* meaning "not," and *otium,* meaning "leisure" or "ease." Taken literally, an individual who is in the process of negotiating is not at ease.

Salary

The ancient Romans knew that salt was a necessary part of a person's diet. To make sure that their army personnel ate enough salt, the Romans paid each soldier a "salt allowance," called *argentum salarium. Argentum* originally meant "silver," but since silver was the basis of much of Roman currency, the term came to mean "money" as well. In time, the Romans dropped *argentum* from the phrase and gradually broadened its meaning to denote any "regular payment for services." Centuries later, English adopted *salarium,* keeping the meaning, but changing the spelling to "salary." *See also* **worth one's salt** *(page 89).*

Tally

Tally is frequently used to express the idea of an account or a score kept either by notches or marks or by figures in books or on sheets of paper. Before the invention of adding machines and computers, it was customary to record debts or business transactions by making notches on a stick of wood. The notched piece of wood was then split down the middle so that those involved in the transaction had an identical record. Whenever an account needed verification or a payment was to be made, the two parts were placed together to see if they "made a tally." "Tally" traces its origin to the Latin noun *talea,* meaning "a cutting of a plant or tree" or "a short stake or bar."

The first person to tally a perfect 10 in an Olympic gymnastics competition was Romanian gymnast Nadia Comaneci.

Tycoon

The English word "tycoon" traces it origins to two Chinese words: *ta,* which means "great," and *guan,* which means "high official" or "dignitary." The connection between the two languages, however, is not so direct. The Japanese were the first to adopt the Chinese phrase for "great dignitary." English-speaking travelers in East Asia first heard the Chinese phrase *taguan* when spoken by the Japanese, who pronounced it *taikan.* The Japanese, however, were using it to refer to the shogun, the hereditary military leader of an area. Speakers of English who visited the area and heard *taikan* soon adapted it to "tycoon" and used it to refer to Japanese shoguns. Gradually, "tycoon" adopted a second, more commonly used meaning—a powerful, rich industrial leader.

Fantastic Foreigners

The words in this chapter might seem both foreign and familiar. It's because English has borrowed these words from other languages, either partially or "lock, stock, and barrel" (to borrow from Chapter 5's exceptional expressions).

Ad hoc

The purpose of an ad hoc committee is to focus on a specific situation and discuss ways to resolve the problem involved. *Ad* and *hoc* are Latin words meaning "to" and "this." Thus, an ad hoc committee on interstate highway speed limits would study the pros and cons of lowering or raising existing speed limits.

The *curia* was the name of the Roman Senate house. It could accommodate 600 senators. Since there were no platforms, senators merely stood up to speak.

Adios/Vaya con Dios

Both expressions, heard frequently now in the United States, are Spanish phrases meaning goodbye. Their literal translation, however, means much more. "Adios" is actually a combination of the two Spanish words *a* and *dios* meaning "to God." *Vaya con Dios* translates "may you go with God."

Al fresco

The Italian *al fresco* means "in the cool." For centuries, especially before air conditioning, Italians enjoyed eating their meals in the cool outdoor air. The practice continues today, as many restaurants throughout Italy offer their patrons the option of a table outdoors. Although "al fresco" originally referred to eating outdoors, today it refers to any event that takes place outdoors.

Apropos

The French term *à propos* literally translates as "to the purpose." In English it is spelled as one word and means "at the right time" or "relevant."

Bon voyage

Shouts of "bon voyage" can be heard as passengers leave on a trip. Literally translated from French to English as "good voyage," it expresses the wish for a pleasant journey.

Bouquet

"Bouquet" is derived from the Old French *bosquet,* meaning "thicket." In English a bouquet describes a bundle of flowers or a fragrant smell.

Bravo

"Bravo" is frequently used to express admiration for a job well done. The word traces its origin to an unlikely ancestor—the Latin adjective *barbarus,* referring to an uncivilized, crude foreigner.

Chutzpah

"Chutzpah" is a colloquial Yiddish term meaning "insolence" and "boldness." Although "chutzpah" was originally used to refer to something done with incredible disrespect, the term has begun to lose its negative meaning. Now it is most often used to refer to the guts it takes to do something.

Yiddish is a language based on medieval Rhineland German, which was spoken by the Jews in eastern, northern, and central Europe. Yiddish has Hebrew, Russian, and Polish elements and uses Hebrew characters. Yiddish is still spoken and read today, though by smaller numbers of people.

Dolce vita

Composers and writers often write about *la dolce vita.* This Italian phrase, which translates into "the sweet life," means just that— a life that is without cares or concerns. When used sarcastically, it implies an immoral way of living and one that is devoted to pleasure.

Gung ho

This is actually an English adaptation of the Chinese phrase *gong he,* meaning "work together." Used often in informal or everyday speech, the expression refers to people who are enthusiastic, creative, and eager to involve themselves completely in some project.

During World War II, U.S. Marine officer Evans Carlson was commander of the 2nd Marine Raider Battalion in the Pacific. When speaking of the forces he commanded, he referred to them as the Gung Ho Battalion, meaning that they were enthusiastic and all worked together.

Kowtow

In English, "kowtow" is often used sarcastically when speaking of the behavior of a person who acts as a slave to another person. *Kowtow,* or *ketou,* is actually Chinese for "knock the head." For centuries, Chinese individuals would kneel before their superiors and knock their head to the floor as a sign of respect. This custom applied to everyone. Even foreign ambassadors had to kowtow to the emperor.

Laissez faire

This theory maintains that government should not interfere in economic affairs, but should leave the economy to naturally reach its peak. It is also referred to as "hands-off" economics, and literally translates to "to let [people] do as they please."

Latin Expressions

Latin is the root language for many languages. Here are some Latin words or phrases that have entered into English verbatim (or with no change in spelling):

Expression	Meaning
Ad infinitum	to an infinite degree
Alter ego	another self
Anno domini (A.D.)	in the year of the Lord
Ante meridiem (A.M.)	before the middle of the day
Carpe diem	sieze the day
Exempli gratia (e.g.)	for the sake of example
Id est (i.e.)	that is
In loco parentis	in place of a parent
In situ	in the proper situation
Magnum opus	the chief work of an author or musician
Modus operandi	the mode of working
Modus vivendi	the manner of living
Post meridiem (P.M.)	after the middle of the day
Pro bono	for the good
Quid pro quo	an equal exchange or substitution
Requiescat in pace (RIP)	may he/she rest in peace
Semper paratus	always prepared
Tempus fugit	time flies
Terra firma	dry land
Videlicet (viz.)	namely
Vox populi	the voice of the people

Mazel tov

The biblical term *mazel* means "planet," "star," or "sign of the zodiac." Gradually, *mazel* came to mean "a sign of luck." *Tov* is the Hebrew word for "good." In time, the expression "mazel tov" developed. Today, it is frequently heard at weddings and on other joyous occasions to wish someone good luck.

Melee

Its English meaning is "a noisy, confused fight among a number of people." In French *mêlée* literally means "a mixing."

Plaza

Commonly used throughout the United States to describe a public square, marketplace, business center, or mall, "plaza" is actually from Spanish, where it has the same meaning.

The public square in Greek city-states was known as the *agora*. It was an open space within the city that was the center of civic life.

Presto

When the Italians want something done as quickly as possible, they often use the word *presto.* English readily adopted this word, which traces its roots to the Latin verb *praestare,* meaning "to guarantee" or "to be responsible for something."

Protege

In English, the word means "a person guided or helped in his or her career by a more influential person." The French *protégé* translates to "protected."

RSVP

Ever notice the four initials RSVP at the bottom of an invitation? Each is the initial letter of a word in the French phrase *repondez, s'il vous plait,* which translates to "answer, if you please." So, the next time you receive a request for your presence at a party, follow proper **etiquette** (another French word, for proper manners) and respond, please.

According to etiquette expert Amy Vanderbilt, one should immediately respond to an invitation with a handwritten note on conservative stationery.

Salud

This Spanish exclamation translates literally "Health!" It is frequently said at celebrations and on festive occasions when guests raise their glasses and drink to the good luck, health, and happiness of others. "Salud" traces its roots to the ancient Latin noun *salus,* also meaning "health."

Sang-froid

One who has sang-froid exhibits cool self-possession or composure (or is cold blooded), especially in trying circumstances. *Sang* is French for "blood," and *froid* is French for "cold."

Savoir-faire

This French expression is commonly used in English to express a person's tactfulness, especially his or her readiness to say the right words or do the right things. The phrase, which translates literally as "to know [how] to do," traces its roots to two Latin verbs, *sapere* ("to know") and *facere* ("to do" or "to make").

Sayonara

"Sayonara" is actually a compound of two Japanese words, *sayo*, meaning "that way," and *nara*, meaning "if." Literally translated the expression means "if it is to be that way." For the Japanese, *sayonara* means not only "be well," but also "until we meet again." English adopted the word to mean "goodbye."

Shalom

A term used worldwide by Jews and others to mean both "hello" and "goodbye," *shalom* literally means "peace." Its use also implies a wish for good health, success, and happiness.

Shalom aleichem, or "peace be with you," is one of the warmest and sincerest greetings a Jewish person can offer.

Siesta

Daytime in ancient Rome was divided into 12 hours, beginning at 6 A.M. Accordingly, noon was known as the *sexta hora,* or "sixth hour." In Spain, where noon is the hottest part of the day, it became a common practice for people to take a rest, sometimes even a nap, at this time. Gradually, the term "siesta" came to describe the resting period just after noon.

Tête-à-tête

These French words literally translate to "head-to-head." In English, a tête-à-tête is a private or intimate conversation between two people.

Viva, viva

Cries of "Viva, viva!" might echo through the streets of Italy, Portugal, and Spain as a motorcade accompanies a reigning king or newly elected president. The same cry often greets a champion athlete after a match or the conductor of an orchestra after a brilliant performance. In English, *viva* translates as "long live"— quite appropriate since its root is the Latin verb *vivere,* meaning "to live."

Index

baptize (bap-TIEZ), 45
barbarian (bahr-BEYR-ee-an), 18
basin (BEY-sin), 101
battle, 166
beauty (BEEYU-tee), 180
beef up, 71
belfry (BEL-free), 46
belligerent (be-LIJ-er-ent), 166
besiege (bi-SEEJ), 167
beware a wolf in sheep's
  clothing, 71
beware of Greeks bearing gifts, 72
beyond the pale, 72
Bible (BIE-bel), 46
bill, 198
bin, 101
biology (bie-OL-o-jee), 134
blitzkrieg (BLITS-kreeg), 167
bobby (BOB-ee), 154
bonsai (BAWN-zie), 134
bon voyage
  (bohn vwah-YAHZH), 204
bouquet (bow-KAY), 205
bravo (BRAH-voe), 205
Brazil (bra-ZIL), 19
buccaneer (buk-a-NIHR), 167
buckle (BUK-el), 92
buckram (BUK-ram), 94
budget (BUJ-it), 199
buff, 93
bugle (BEEYU-gel), 168
bungalow (BUNG-ga-low), 102

C

caftan (KAF-tan), 93
calabash (KAL-a-bash), 102
caliph (KAY-lif), 47
call a spade a spade, 73
calligraphy (ka-LIG-ra-fee), 3
camp, 118
canal, 19
canary (ka-NEHR-ee), 135
Candice (KAN-dis), 181
candidate (KAN-di-dayt), 154
candy, 103

cane, 103
canopy (KAN-o-pee), 103
capital (KAP-i-tal), 168
captain (KAP-ten), 168
carat (KAR-et), 193
caravan (KAR-a-van), 126
carpe diem (KAHR-pay DEE-um), 207
carry-all, 126
cartel (kahr-TEL), 199
castle (KAS-el)168
cataract (KAT-a-rakt), 19
catch a Tartar, 73
cemetery (SEM-a-ter-ee), 47
center (SEN-ter), 33
chair, 104
chapel (CHAP-el), 2
chaplain (CHAP-len), 2
checkmate (CHEK-mayt), 119
chew the fat, 74
chiaroscuro (kee-ahr-o-SKOOR-oe), 4
chiclets (CHIK-lets), 104
china (CHI-na), 105
chisel (CHIZ-el), 105
choleric (KOL-e-rik), 38
chop chop, 80
chop suey, 105
chow mein (CHOU MAYN), 105
Christian (KRIS-chen), 47
chukker (CHUK-er), 119
chutzpah (KHOOTS-pa), 205
citizen (SIT-e-zen), 154
city, 154
civics, (SIV-iks), 154
civil (SIV-el), 154
civilization (siv-e-le-ZAY-shen), 154
claustrophobia
  (claws-tro-FOE-bee-a), 191
cloister (KLOIS-ter), 47
cloth, 94
coast, 20
cocoa (KOE-koe), 106
colonel (KUR-nel), 169
comet (KOM-it), 34
companion (kom-PAN-yen), 181
company (KUM-pa-nee), 181

genie (JEE-nee), 50
geography (jee-OG-ra-fee), 21
geology (jee-OL-o-jee), 37
geometry (jee-OM-e-tree), 37
geyser (GIE-zer), 135
girl, 21
gladiator (glad-ee-A-tor), 136
gladiolus (glad-ee-OE-les), 136
glamour (GLAM-er), 184
glossary (GLOS-a-ree), 5
go berserk (go ber-SURK), 77
govern (GUV-ern), 157
grand vizier (grand VI-zihr), 158
graphic (GRAF-ik), 5
Greek fire, 170
grenade (gre-NAYD), 170
grin like a Cheshire cat, 77
guerrilla (ge-RIL-a), 171
guillotine (GIL-o-teen), 158
gum, 136
gun, 171
gung ho, 206
guru (GOOW-roow), 51
gymnastics (jim-NAS-tiks), 119

H

hacienda (hah-see-EN-da), 108
halcyon days (HAL-see-on days), 51
harem (HEYR-em), 22
hazard (HAZ-erd), 184
hearse (hurs), 184
heckler (HEK-ler), 185
hectic (HEK-tik), 185
heresy (HER-i-see), 52
heretic (HER-i-tik), 52
hieroglyphs (HIE-er-o-glifs), 146
histrionics (his-tree-ON-iks), 186
horoscope (HOR-o-skowp), 193
hospital (HOS-pi-tel), 37
humor (HYOOW-mor), 38
humorous (HYOOW-mor-us), 38
hydrophobia (hie-dro-FOE-bee-a), 191
hypocrite (HIP-o-krit), 186
hysteria (hi-STER-ee-a), 187

I

ibis (IE-bis), 137
icon, 52
iconoclast (IE-kon-o-klast), 52
idea (ie-DEE-a), 187
ideal (ie-DEE-al), 187
id est (i.e.) (id EST), 207
idiot (ID-ee-ot), 187
immortal (i-MORT-l), 52
imperial (im-PIHR-ee-al), 156
imperious (im-PIHR-ee-us), 156
impress (im-PRES), 12
incunabula (in-kyoow-NAB-yu-la), 6
India ink (IN-dee-a ingk), 6
infant, 22
infantry (IN-fan-tree), 172
in loco parentis
    (in LOE-koe pa-REN-tis), 207
innocent (IN-o-sent), 188
in situ (in SI-too), 207
intrigue (IN-treeg), 188
inundate (IN-un-dayt), 188
invent, 38
iron curtain, 158
Islam (IS-lahm), 53
italics (i-TAL-iks), 6

J

jade (jayd), 137
Janus-faced (JAY-nus-fayst), 53
jeopardy (JEP-ar-dee), 189
jewels (JOOW-els), 96
jig is up, 78
jodhpurs (JOD-purs), 96
journal (JUR-nel), 127
journey (JUR-nee), 127
jovial (JOE-vee-al), 189
jubilee (JU-ba-lee), 54
judo (JU-doe), 120
juggernaut (JUG-er-not), 55
jujitsu (JU-jit-soo), 120
jungle, 138
jury, 159

The Indo-European

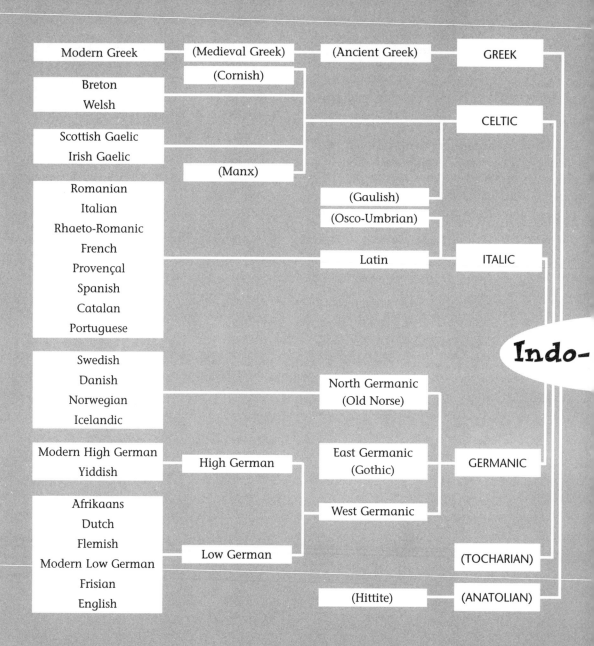

Modern Greek — (Medieval Greek) — (Ancient Greek) — GREEK

(Cornish)

Breton
Welsh

CELTIC

Scottish Gaelic
Irish Gaelic

(Manx)

Romanian
Italian
Rhaeto-Romanic
French
Provençal
Spanish
Catalan
Portuguese

(Gaulish)
(Osco-Umbrian)
Latin — ITALIC

Swedish
Danish
Norwegian
Icelandic

North Germanic
(Old Norse)

Modern High German
Yiddish

High German

East Germanic
(Gothic)

GERMANIC

Afrikaans
Dutch
Flemish
Modern Low German
Frisian
English

Low German

West Germanic

(TOCHARIAN)

(Hittite) — (ANATOLIAN)

Indo-

Languages in parentheses are obsolete.

Family of Languages

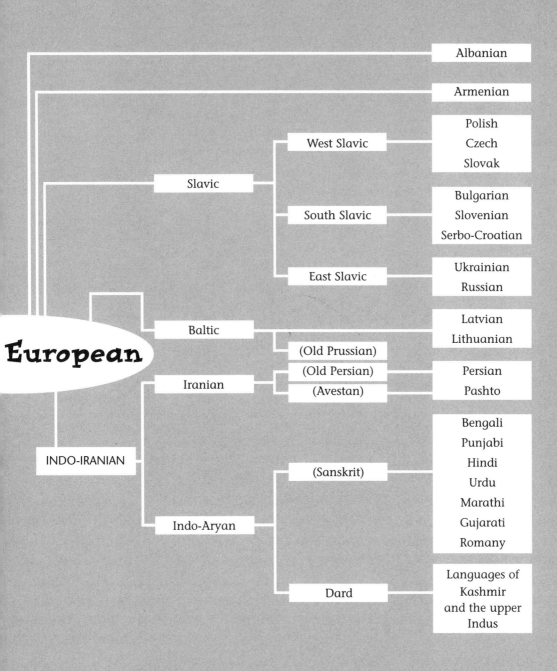

Albanian

Armenian

Slavic
- West Slavic: Polish, Czech, Slovak
- South Slavic: Bulgarian, Slovenian, Serbo-Croatian
- East Slavic: Ukrainian, Russian

Baltic: Latvian, Lithuanian
(Old Prussian)

European

Iranian
- (Old Persian): Persian
- (Avestan): Pashto

INDO-IRANIAN

Indo-Aryan
- (Sanskrit): Bengali, Punjabi, Hindi, Urdu, Marathi, Gujarati, Romany
- Dard: Languages of Kashmir and the upper Indus

Rosalie Baker has been collecting word stories for more than 20 years as the co-editor (with her husband Charles) of *Calliope*, the world history magazine for young people. Her monthly column, "Fun With Words," has kept readers entertained and informed with its lively look at words and how they are used today. She is an authority on classical civilizations and classical and Romance languages, and served as head of the foreign language department for the New Bedford, Massachusetts, public school system. She is also the author of seven books on ancient civilizations and is the editor of the children's archaeology magazine *Dig*.

Tom Lopes' slightly off-center illustrations have been a regular part of the "Fun With Words" column in *Calliope* magazine for years. Tom works as an editorial cartoonist for the New Bedford, MA, *Standard-Times* and the *South Coast Insider*. He is also a private art instructor and restores furniture and art. He lives in Fairhaven, Massachusetts. See more at *www.tomlopes.com*.